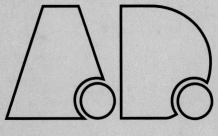

ARCHITECTURAL DESIGN

EDITORIAL OFFICES:
42 LEINSTER GARDENS, LONDON W2 3AN
TEL: 071-402 2141 FAX: 071-723 9540

EDITOR: Maggie Toy
EDITORIAL TEAM: Rachel Bean,
Katherine MacInnes
ART EDITOR: Andrea Bettella
CHIEF DESIGNER: Mario Bettella
DESIGNER: Jan Richter

CONSULTANTS: Catherine Cooke, Terry
Farrell, Kenneth Frampton, Charles Jencks,
Heinrich Klotz, Leon Krier, Robert Maxwell,
Demetri Porphyrios, Kenneth Powell, Colin
Rowe, Derek Walker

SUBSCRIPTION OFFICES:
UK: VCH PUBLISHERS (UK) LTD
8 WELLINGTON COURT, WELLINGTON STREET
CAMBRIDGE CB1 1HZ
TEL: (0223) 321111 FAX: (0223) 313321

USA AND CANADA: VCH PUBLISHERS INC
303 NW 12TH AVENUE DEERFIELD BEACH,
FLORIDA 33442-1788 USA
TEL: (305) 428-5566 / (800) 367-8249
FAX: (305) 428-8201

ALL OTHER COUNTRIES:
VCH VERLAGSGESELLSCHAFT MBH
BOSCHSTRASSE 12, POSTFACH 101161
69451 WEINHEIM
FEDERAL REPUBLIC OF GERMANY
TEL: 06201 606 148 FAX: 06201 606 184

D1228956

CONTENTS

Sir Denys Lasdun, The Hallfield School, London, 1951

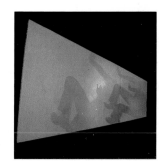

Matthew Barnett Howland, The Wall, 1994

Regent's Park, London's landscape/parkland inside the city

GUY BATTLE AND CHRISTOPHER McCARTHY
MULTI-SOURCE SYNTHESIS
The Design of Sustainable New Towns

By the 21st century 70 to 80 per cent of the world's population will live in concentrated urban centres. Nowhere is the demand for new towns going to be greater than in the developing world. As technology renders the field worker redundant and as population increases, more and more people will migrate away from their rural settlements to the urban centres, demanding housing, feeding, higher standards of living and thereby increasing pollution and placing greater demands on the world's already depleted natural resources.

To find the solution, we must first ask the right questions, for example, 'What are cities, how do they work?' Cities and towns are a complex mesh of people, lifestyles, machines, buildings, politics, power. However, from a purely engineering basis, they can be more simply defined as systems that import raw materials (input) to fuel a 'metabolism', that exports goods (output) and refuse material (waste).

This 'metabolism' can be fairly accurately defined in terms of input, useful output and waste, using a simple accounting and balance sheet. Typically a metabolic balance sheet would indicate that the actual useful product is small compared with the input (ie often less than 1%). Such studies also show the vast amount of waste that is typically put directly back into the biosphere (approximately 70%). In many cases, this goes back as raw pollution, leaving the biosphere to 'absorb' and process it for us. Following this philosophy, the earth can be viewed as a series of reservoirs (for resource) and sinks (for waste), both the reservoirs and sinks having finite capacity. At present rates the reservoir will quickly become empty and the sink full. It is therefore necessary to identify the various processes that go on to make up this metabolism so that their efficiencies can be improved, not only as individual cycles but also in the manner in which they can beneficially interact. There are two basic ways to view a city's metabolism. Either as a linear process, (input gives output plus waste) or as a cyclical process that produces feed back loops and recycles wastes. The key difference between these two viewpoints is that the linear system will eventually reach full capacity, whereas the circular system is sustainable.

The system can be identified by the following

characteristics – *Linear*: water use high and is polluted; sewage is discarded; toxic fumes pollute; building materials and 'wastes'; trees felled without replacement. *Circular*: low water consumption, treated and recycled; wastes reused for fertiliser, heating and energy; fossil fuel used efficiently; building materials recycled and used discarded; trees replanted.

Any city can be designed (or evolve) from two starting points. That is the smallest module outward (ie building – streets – urban clusters – city, eg London) or from a strategic level inwards (macro planning, street scape, city blocks, buildings eg Manhattan). In most historic cases, this has been a process of evolution. London grew from a series of small clusters to become a massive urban conurbation, with the transportation and water systems being added as a result of growth (micro – macro). In contrast, Manhattan, grew from an initial orthogonal planning grid (macro – micro). But essentially both are the results of evolution rather than any real strategy, and thus the metabolism is generally linear rather than cyclical (eg refuse is rarely used to provide energy, it is merely transported out to sea and dumped as in the case of Manhattan). Indeed, both London and New York in comparison to many other 'mega' cities are extremely wasteful, producing 950 tonnes of rubbish per year per person compared to Mexico City which produces only 350 tonnes per person per year (a reflection on an affluent and effluent rich society!). However, within the developing world, with the ever increasing demand for new housing and new towns, neither approach has proved to produce an ideal result. The only real way to design sustainable cities is by being able to effect (ie design) both the macro and micro levels of the town simultaneously. For instance, it is no good designing an efficient energy production system if all buildings are going to be air conditioned and profligate energy users. Thus, it is absolutely essential that the designer (urban planner) has some means of regulating the amount of energy any building plot may use by legislation or guidelines. This does not mean that there would be a heavier handed planning approach, merely that there would be a more rigorous set of guidelines and targets for the designers to work to, encouraging them to

ABOVE: Stockpile of cattle bones; Early inhabitants of the Galapagos Islands introduced horses as a means of transport, with little regard for the environmental consequences

FROM ABOVE L TO R: Beehive; New York City;
Travelling Buddhist priest

III

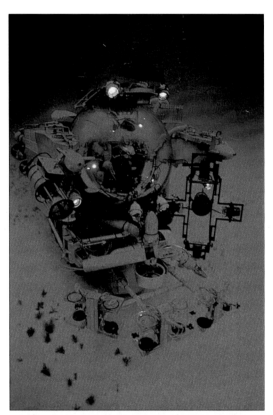

FROM ABOVE L TO R: Johnson Sea-link Submersible can descend to 1000m (3000 ft) from a surface support ship; Nutrient laden water supports plankton that feeds millions of fish; Snake hatching

maximise energy efficiency in return for floor area. Within existing cities, this is notoriously difficult to achieve. However, in the developing world, where new towns on green field sites are more common place, then such an approach is viable and essential for the well-being and balance of the earth.

A formula for sustainable development

A town's metabolism is comprised of six cycles which each have their own individual patterns but in some way all affect one another: transportation; energy; water; waste; micro climate, landscape and ecology; materials, construction and buildings. Naturally, many of the decisions to be made with respect to the above, are site specific and would necessarily take into account fundamental factors, such as: the climate (solar, temperature, humidity, precipitation, wind) ; geology (site conditions, materials resources, topology); location; economics of country, etc. However, in many cases the general objectives remain the same.

Sustainable transportation

This can be defined as transport which aids the mobility of one generation without compromising the mobility of future generations. Clearly many of today's transportation modes are not in keeping with this definition: the private car – the first choice of many in the developed world – is one of the major causes of the current high levels of pollution in our urban areas and in many places automobile accidents are the major cause of death in the under 50 age group.

Whilst the developed world is only now beginning to realise the irredeemable damage the car has done to society in terms of land-take, inner city deterioration, accident levels, air quality and noise, for the rapidly modernising and expanding economies of the developing world the problems are only just beginning. Rapidly increasing car ownership levels coupled with climatic humidity may soon mean that in many industrialising countries, environmental pollution indicators may soon exceed those currently being experienced in the industrialised nations. The challenge therefore is to prevent this foreseeable disaster from actually occurring without denying citizens of the developing world the indisputable benefits which increased personal mobility, facilitated by the car, can bring.

The key to a sustainable transportation system is the implementation of a transport hierarchy which gives priority to the pedestrian and public systems above the car. This does not necessarily imply positive discrimination against the private car: successful implementation of such a hierarchy can be achieved by merely creating an environment which does not cater for the car. This can be accomplished by limited

parking spaces, traffic calming, cheap mass transit and by establishing a network of roads unsuitable for vehicular traffic: pedestrian; cycle based; mass transit (public); car. The hierarchy chosen will dictate which modes have 'design' priority over others. Successful implementation of such a structure will depend upon a segregated environment and will fundamentally effect design decisions. The dominance of the car is based on its convenience. In order to encourage people to use public network and then walk (or cycle) it is important that the system must be of a high quality and provide similar or better service.

An acceptable walking distance within any town is about 150–300m or 5–10 mins maximum. Thus any mass transit system and urban plan should be based around this module. If walking is essential then pedestrian (and cycle) routes must be carefully planned to be scenic with good views; shaded from sun and passively cooled; streets narrow enough to provide shade; protection from rain; interaction with wild life and effect on the fauna.

There are two options for mass transit: high speed with large stop spacing (monorail) needing secondary modes such as taxis to cover intermediate distances ; or slower speed (LRT, trolley bus) providing a comprehensive coverage to negate the need for other modes (except walking). Costs depend largely on the ground conditions and topography, however a broad cost comparison is as follows: Monorail $132m-$360m; LRT $48m-$162m; Trolley bus $19m-$25m.

Phasing is an essential element of any choice for it will effect timing and the magnitude of costs. One of the major perceived advantages of rail based (LRT) systems is this huge up front capital investment required, with no opportunity to accrue revenue until they are fully operational, despite the fact that environmentally and urbanistically they have great advantages. It is therefore essential to examine the possible phasing of such a system to achieve the same end goal: roads constructed for a bus system (Bio diesel); bus upgraded to 'trolley bus' (electricity produced from waste or CHP); profits used to fund rail infrastructure; light rail system (LRT) installed (clear electricity control over country roads can be pedestrianised).

Energy

Energy in the form of electricity, gas, oil is used within three broad categories: buildings 50%; transport 25%; industry 25%. The underlying principle of any energy strategy must be to firstly reduce the demand and secondly to provide the energy required from a renewable source thus creating a self sustaining (and in this case, even self sufficient) system. It is clear however that to achieve this, both the demand

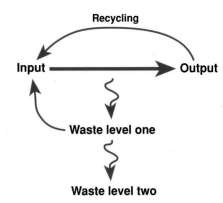

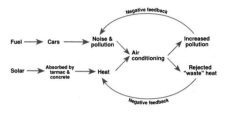

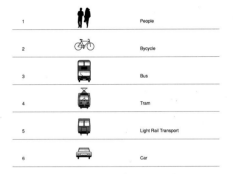

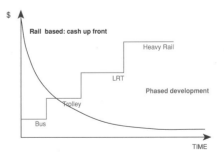

FROM ABOVE: Circular metabolism; Self-propagating use of air conditioning; Two methods of analysing the transportation hierarchy

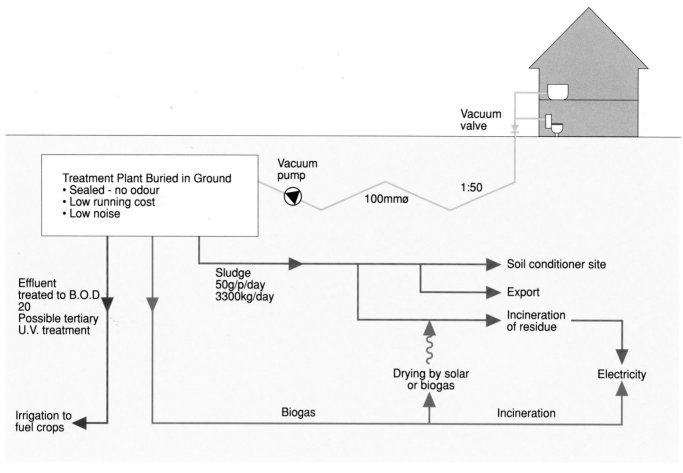

Vacuum valve

Vacuum pump

Treatment Plant Buried in Ground
• Sealed - no odour
• Low running cost
• Low noise

100mmø   1:50

Effluent
treated to B.O.D
20
Possible tertiary
U.V. treatment

Sludge
50g/p/day
3300kg/day

Soil conditioner site

Export

Incineration
of residue

Drying by solar
or biogas

Electricity

Irrigation to
fuel crops

Biogas   Incineration

Waste management

Storage Requirement = 180,000m3
if 0.5m deep then area required is 360,000m2

Given by; canals 14 km x 8m wide
lakes 259,000m2

• Utilise open canals to avoid burying drainage + expensive pipework systems
• Open canals adjacent to paved areas to collect runoff
• Sufficient rainwater falls throughout year to provide needs of town
• Storage required to provide water supply during "dry" periods

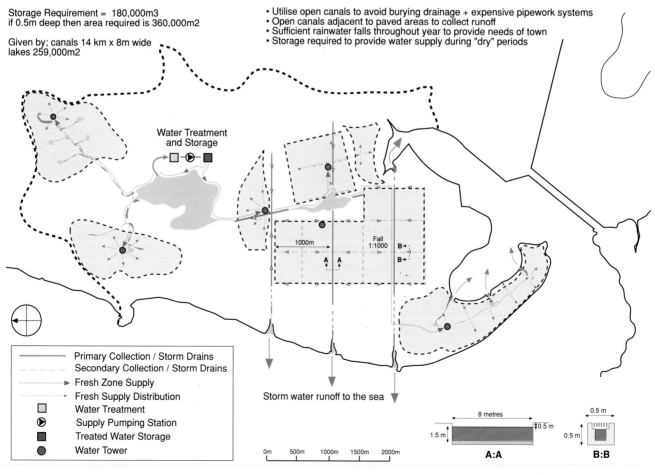

Water Treatment
and Storage

1000m   Fall
1:1000   B

A A   B

Storm water runoff to the sea

—————— Primary Collection / Storm Drains
– – – – – Secondary Collection / Storm Drains
·····▸ Fresh Zone Supply
·····▸ Fresh Supply Distribution
☐ Water Treatment
◉ Supply Pumping Station
■ Treated Water Storage
● Water Tower

0m 500m 1000m 1500m 2000m

8 metres
0.5 m
1.5 m
A:A

0.5 m
0.5 m
B:B

Water and waste management

and supply must be tackled simultaneously and by the same strategic design body.

Building demand can be limited by producing design guidelines and energy targets for given plots of land. Typically, this will influence decision making with respect to both the building systems and architectural response. Importantly, it will place greater emphasis on the architect to develop a building type that is environmentally responsive (or selective) rather than being environment rejecting. Thus buildings will need to be: naturally ventilated wherever feasible; daylit; limit use of air conditioning; utilise solar energy for heating, cooling and ventilation efficient systems; careful orientation and planning; appropriate materials choice. By adopting these principles, it may be possible to reduce the actual energy demand by up to 70%.

Energy is traditionally supplied in three forms, oil, gas and electricity. Both oil and gas used for heating, cooling, etc can only result in reduction in natural resources, and thus are *not* sustainable. Electricity, although traditionally produced by the combustion of oil, gas or coal, can be produced by the combustion or collection of renewable sources such as: incineration of waste or energy crop (Biomass); solar collection (photovoltaic or solar thermal); wind turbines. However, in all of these processes, the efficiency of the actual electricity production is less than 30%, the remainder being lost as heat (usually up a cooling tower). Essential to the achievement of a sustainable energy policy is the use of this 'waste' heat by the utilisation of combined heat and power plants (CHP). The heat can be used not only to provide winter heating and hot water but also (more importantly) as a source for driving absorption cooling machines. In this manner, the energy production process can achieve up to 85% efficiency.

Renewable sources include – *Biomass*: This includes plant materials that may be specifically grown for energy production (fuel crop) as well as organic wastes that will be generated on site. There has been significant progress with respect to the utilisation of energy crops for energy production. Such an approach has significant advantages in developing countries as they utilise local agricultural skills, low first cost implementation – quick to implement (1–2 years for first crop). *Solar energy*: Photovoltaic – utilises solar cells to convert direct sunlight into electricity (dc). They are fairly inefficient, (10–20%) and at the moment costly. *Solar thermal*: Uses solar energy to heat water to produce steam to drive a turbine etc. Used extensively in California – High capital costs, although they have great potential in sunny climates. *Winds*: Tried and tested systems. Their performance can be enhanced by integration into architectural building form. Following this philosophy, all

the new town would be all electric, with all heating, cooling, lighting, cooking, transportation and industrial systems (tram and/or electric cars) being based on electricity supply.

Water: In most countries, water is a valuable and scarce resource. It is thus important that a specific strategy is adapted that sets, as its prime objective, the achievement of a self-sufficient system; reduce demand; collect and store water over days or months to ensure that it is available all year round; treat and distribute water to areas of need efficiently; recycle waste water where possible for use in WCs or landscape. In any site specific area, it is necessary to carefully examine the precipitation and evaporation data. In many areas of the world, although there are long dry periods of little rainfall, there is often enough rainfall over the wet periods of the year to satisfy the yearly demand. However, essential to this strategy is an efficient collection and storage system. A typical balance for a new town development in a tropical climate indicates that enough rain falls through the 'wet' season to satisfy requirements during the dry season. In the example shown the town has been designed around the need to collect and store water in underground areas, tanks and lakes. The tanks form central squares and act as a significant thermal heat sink creating a cool micro climate within their immediate vicinity, whilst the above ground lakes and canals not only provide visual amenity but also a degree of evaporative cooling. In addition the canals from primary routes along which the landscape can be integrated to form pedestrian walkways and wildlife corridors.

Waste: Waste from a typical city can be broadly categorised into four forms: human effluent; bio-degradable/combustible waste (paper, vegetable materials); non-combustible waste (metals, glass etc); toxic waste. It is essential that the waste strategy is set to carefully deal with these four categories and that the 'waste' is not necessarily seen as something to be disposed of but as a resource to be recycled and re-used. Human effluent produces gas for heating/cooling/power, sludge for composting and water for landscaping. Biodegradable/combustible waste can be cleanly combusted to provide power and heat, can provide compost and ash, can be used for road constuction/aggregate. Non-combustible metals (metals, concrete, glass, etc) – can be recycled or sold on to other areas. Toxic waste must be reprocessed by specialist offsite plant. The simplest means of dealing with this is to ensure that all industrial processes are environmentally friendly and their waste can be easily dealt with.

Microclimate

The creation of a 'comfortable' urban micro-

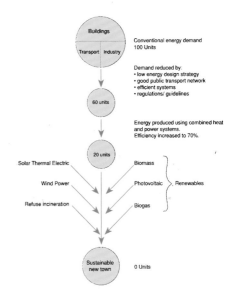

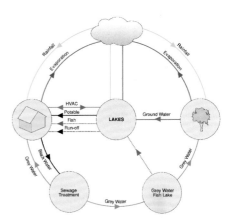

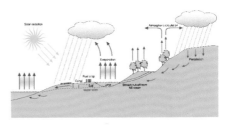

FROM ABOVE: New town energy strategy; Two methods of illustrating the natural water cycle; OPPOSITE FROM ABOVE: Waste management; Water and waste management

climate is essential to the successful operation of the urban transportation strategy of the new town. This will fundamentally affect the planning and layout of the urban environment. The response however will be site specific, primarily responding to the prevailing climate. The climatic elements within the urban area that can be modified by a sensitive urban design include: air temperature and humidities; radiant temperatures (surface) to which occupants are exposed; wind speeds in streets and around buildings; concentration of air pollution within traffic arteries; potential for natural ventilation; shading and potential for daylight; solar exposure and potential for solar energy utilisation. The urban factors that the urban designers have control over and that will effect these aspects are: topographical features of town; density (land cover) of buildings; distances between buildings; orientation and width of streets; urban parks, landscape; colour of buildings and streets; material choice (heavyweight versus lightweight). The aim of adopting such an approach is not to create an even level of comfort throughout the town, which would place too many restrictions on the design, but to create a changing thermal, air quality, acoustic and light 'topography' that recognises the need for varying landscapes. Thus streets may have a combination of fixed and variable shading systems. Bus stops and public squares may have a concentration of evaporative cooling systems (in hot/dry climates such as Seville) or permit good solar penetration (typical northern climate). Landscaping and green areas will play a vital role in the creation of the urbanscape and have a marked influence on the urban environment: provide outdoor shading, protection from cold winds; provide evaporative cooling; absorption of solar radiation; reduction in natural dust and air pollution particles; rainwater absorption; can impede or redirect wind to improve natural ventilation to buildings or surrounding areas. The landscape will also play a vital role in allowing fauna, flora and wildlife a natural path into and through the city. So that the town rather than merely destroying existing habitats can in some cases improve them or introduce new habitats and create opportunities for human and of wildlife interaction.

Materials

The choice of construction materials will play an important part in the sustainability of a new town. The primary objectives being that the materials should be: appropriate to the climate and the climatic response required; of local origin; low embodied energy; utilise local skills for construction; can be recycled; appropriate for the chosen structural regime.

In many cases, new towns comprise two to four storey developments. Although the use of steel or concrete is traditional for these buildings, there are many other alternatives, that in many cases can be sourced locally using local labour. *Stabilised soil blocks*: rammed earth; local soils, made locally; low cost and low embodied energy; can be used up to five or six storeys; recyclable. *Locally fired earth:* clay bricks; local skills; low cost; can be used up to five storeys. *Timber*: low cost, easy to use; sourced locally; replenishable source; low embodied energy; recyclable; *Fibre Concrete* tiling (roofing); uses local materials (coconut and mud or cement). *Risk Hush Ash* (RHA); used to manufacture cement; burnt to provide energy and ash (100 tonnes rice = 5 tonnes ash).

Design Strategy

The very nature of this approach means that at first , each of these cycles should be analysed independently of each other and the urban plan in order to idealise their operation. It is then possible to create a multilayered design which is made up of all the individual components including the urban objectives. They can then be moulded together to create a working metabolism. This design process will involve highlighting the areas of both positive and negative interaction, leading to an emphasis of certain areas, that will inform the urban and architectural design. Thus, the plan for water may highlight a need for open lakes or canals, which can then be utilised as part of the landscape plan, and form an important element of the urban streetscape. Or the transport requirements for drop off points every 300m could form a module upon which the urban centres are clustered, which in turn may tie in with the requirement for water storage, etc.

In this manner, the urban planner, the architect and the engineers can work together with the various specialists to create an integrated plan and strategy based upon informed decision making. This approach to urban design is, however, more involved and more complex than the traditional methodologies for it involves examining the problem in not merely two r three dimensions, but in seven or eight dimensions. All towns and cities have metabolisms, that ultimately form part of the global eco-system. These metabolic cycles must respond to the demands for increased efficiency interaction so that they become sustainable Urban Environmental Design separates, idealises and the recombines these component cycles of the metabolism creating an environment and ecological topography that better satisfies todays demands for cleaner and better cities – *Towards a sustainable future.*

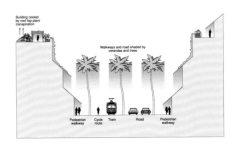

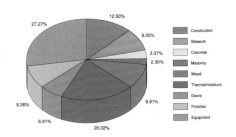

FROM ABOVE: Microclimate; Typical embodied energy in housing; OPPOSITE FROM ABOVE: Autonomous Living Capsule; Kayangez Atoll, Palau, Pacific Ocean.
Thanks to: The Ngiom Partnership; Energy for Sustainable Development; University of London, Centre for Sustainable Development, The Martin Centre, Cambridge

SIR DENYS LASDUN

THE HALLFIELD SCHOOL, LONDON, 1951

The Hallfield School in Paddington was built in 1951 when Sir Denys Lasdun was in his early 30s. The building was commissioned by the London County Council to house 720 children of Infant to Junior School age. Its unique solution to the question of an appropriate design for school architecture is acknowledged in an article headed 'They Built a Brave New World for Children' which claims that 'Its plans-on-paper set so much talk buzzing that architects from such design-conscious countries as Germany, Switzerland and America came over to see it being built'.[1] Mr MW Williams, the first headmaster of the Junior school and a man Lasdun much admired, described the school as 'almost futuristic in design . . . It's a fantastic place. It takes your breath away doesn't it? It is the most exciting school in the country.'[2]

Lasdun's desire to seek new solutions was encouraged by the atmosphere of progressive optimism amongst those responsible for the construction of buildings for education after the Second World War. Andrew Saint suggests that this atmosphere was the result of a puritan strain in British philosophy and design influenced by the Modern Movement, the needs, constraints, opportunities and organisation of post-war reconstruction and the triumph of fresh thought about childhood, teaching and learning.[3] An education act arose from a strong political consensus to provide wider opportunities for everyone. Stuart Maclure describes the new progressive style of education with 'its emphasis on life-enhancing personal development [and] its determination to link cognitive and affective learning in a rich and satisfying synthesis'.[4] Architects were thus responsible for crystallising and articulating new ideals of pedagogy. Lasdun acknowledges that he 'felt very different after the war'. He had won a competition for a school building (unbuilt) with Wells Coates in the 1930s but the formal orthogonal grid solution that he used then is dramatically different from the anti-diagrammatic, anti-institutional nature of the Hallfield School design 20 years later.

The Hallfield Estate in which the school is situated was designed by Tecton. This firm was formed in1931 by the Russian-born Modernist, Berthold Lubetkin with six newly qualified young architects including Lasdun, who became a partner after the war. The firm was dissolved in 1948 and Lasdun and Lindsay Drake carried the Hallfield project through to its completion. Though they were responsible for the further development of the plan, the basic organisation and design, except for the school, date from before 1948. The dissolution of Tecton was a pivotal point in Lasdun's career. The contrast between the modular housing scheme of the estate designed by Tecton in the tradition of Le Corbusier's 'Unité de Habitation', and Lasdun's subsequent rejection of universal formalism in his design for the school, indicate that the dissolution of Tecton also marked the beginning of Lasdun's mature style. Indeed he developed themes in the design of the Hallfield School that have become hallmarks of his architecture.

The organic, elongated layout of the Junior School, anticipates the distribution of buildings for the University of East Anglia project in 1963. Both shapes are dictated by site. Hallfield School is on an axis which marks a contrast with the grid of the estate and it fits into the triangle of land which was left when it was decided to reduce the density of buildings by removing two housing blocks from the Tecton plan. The original gardens are thought to have been landscaped by Loudon and many of the mature trees are incorporated in the scheme for the school. At East Anglia Lasdun also grafted the buildings to the natural features echoing the contours of the landscape, and orientating them according to their prospect and aspect.

The school is designed as a 'small world for children in which their needs and interests were the overriding factor'.[5] The building has low ceilings and the hexagonal windows in the corridor of the Infant School are at an adult's knee height. The curved corridors fuel the imagination and give the impression of a wealth of interesting possibilities around each bend. This concept has been developed in Lasdun's later work to incorporate a similar theme on a much larger scale, namely the *promenade architecturale* where buildings are treated as a microcosm of the city. He explains – 'The things that are pleasurable in cities: the parks, the rivers, the trees, the streets, the passages the bridges the people wandering around, I mean that is what is fun, amusing and interesting because it arouses people's curiosity. Buildings

FROM ABOVE: A pupil wearing a cap with the school badge which adopted the plan of the school building as its logo; One of a 'cluster' of pavilions that comprise the Infant School showing their proximity to the garden; OPPO-SITE: Entrance of school showing the blue glass surrounding the water tank on the roof of the administration department

have a parallel. What the parks, streets and bridges are to a city, halls, passages and vestibules are to a building and I like to move people through a building in the same way that they move through a city. Not a city on a grid but a city like London which has grown up organically over time and yet there is an architectural control behind it.'[6]

One of the most innovative aspects of the Hallfield School is this scaling down of space to achieve a feeling of security and informality in stark contrast to the impersonal spaces that comprised daunting educational institutions of the past. Writing in 1965, Lasdun claims that 'Architecture expresses itself primarily through the quintessential medium of space . . . The significance of space as we move through it is that, like language, it is to be delighted in. And, like language, space can be formal, informal, warm, cold, public or private, high or low status'.[7] Lasdun achieves a feeling of protection as one progresses from the public space of the estate to the increasingly closed world of the school but simultaneously the plan inspires a feeling of curiosity encouraging adventure. That the children have responded to this tailored design can, to a certain extent, be gauged from 'The "remarkable" attendance of at least 90 percent of the pupils' described by the headmaster at the prize giving to mark the end of the first year as the 'most outstanding feature of the year'.[8]

The successful realisation of Lasdun's aim to make a 'second home for the pupils' can be attributed to what is perhaps one of the most characteristic features of his later work – 'something that still interests me enormously – how to give a feeling of enclosure without making a wall'. He points out that the solution – to project an overhanging ceiling and make the 'walls' glass from floor to ceiling – was later used in the National Theatre (1965) to great effect. Lasdun calls this 'deep space architecture' and the shadows that are created by the extended soffits and gaping recesses, are an important part of the design. This solution also achieves a close relationship between inside and out: 'it is not a wall with a window in it, it is a great ceiling which goes out and gives protection.' The Infant School at Hallfield is below street level and the glass 'walls' allow dappled light to penetrate the class room and permit views onto banks of wild grasses and flower beds.

The Infant and Junior Schools are structurally independent of each other, except for a linking glass corridor. This feature has been praised by the teaching staff as it allows the activities of each school to be staggered, engendering the security experienced in smaller groups and encouraging maximum use of outside space. The plan consists of a double curve, the outer

one of two storeys is the Junior School which curls protectively around the cluster of pavilions that house the Infant School: 'I call the whole thing a cluster – a very early example of clustering in other words breaking blocks down away from diagrams into smaller pieces, in order to allow maximum light, space and views'.[9] The cluster is perhaps one of the concepts for which Lasdun is best remembered. He used it in the design of cluster-block social housing in Bethnal Green 1952-54, one example of which, Keeling House, has been listed recently.

Rather than using the geometry of Corbusier's 'Radiant City', Lasdun uses biological analogues to conceptualise his schemes and he designed the cluster blocks using pods and stems as his starting point. One of the first examples of this approach can be seen in the botanical sketch which parallels the Hallfield plan. Lasdun has described his buildings as organisms, at once 'complete and incomplete'. While the Hallfield School is more complete than most of his subsequent work, it includes a 'budding point' on the apex of the Junior School entrance. In July 1956 the LCC decided to add a further four classrooms to the Junior School for which Lasdun added an annex on the axis of this budding point.

The hexagonal pitched roofs of this annexe were designed in collaboration with the Timber Development Association but the main structure of the school is concrete. Lasdun realised the importance of collaborative design especially since extensive use of precast concrete was in its experimental stages at this point. Features such as the shapely two storey precast concrete mullions on the southern face of the Junior School which are placed in such a way as to prevent glare from the continuous external glazing, were designed in collaboration with Arups. It was reported at the time that 'close collaboration between the architect and engineer has resulted in an economical structural system [which is] fundamentally an exploitation of all the possible load bearing elements'.[10] The cost of £120 – £130,000 was considered to be very reasonable at the time. As with the National Theatre, the school needs maintenance. In defence of the theatre, Lasdun explains 'if a person's face is gnarled like mine, you accept it . . . but dirt and rust are inexcusable . . . concrete has become a cliché for attack but we must learn to look with concrete-friendly eyes'.[11]

The concrete at the Hallfield School is unpainted but bright colours in the form of yellow jointless flooring and red quarry tiles were introduced at points of focus where a child's eye might come to rest and a mural was commissioned for the entrance hall. A water tank encased in cobalt blue glass, positioned on top of the administrative block, is one of the school's

FROM ABOVE: Double storey concrete mullions of the Junior School; Curved outside wall of the assembly hall

most engaging features. The tank is functional in that gravity assists the transfer of water from this high point, but, by encasing it in blue glass, Lasdun also made it beautiful. These two qualities seem to me to embody the design concept of the whole school. It was probably the first school designed to appear as the natural focus of the internal life of a residential neighbourhood. Its success in this role is, perhaps, best demonstrated by the fact that the school chose to use the plan of the building as the logo for their school badge.

It is interesting to conclude by drawing a comparison between today's approach to school architecture and that of the 50s when the Hallfield School was erected. Frank Duffy, President of the RIBA chose Woodlea School in Hampshire as the 'RIBA Building of the Year 1994'. Duffy justified his decision by saying that the set up was exceptional in that the 'architects and educationalists did not tolerate the national minimum as the notional standard, but rather, searching for excellence, declared that the children using this school deserve the best.' He asked 'how much finer life in this country would be if housing and architects' departments had been allowed to raise standards cumulatively and continuously'. As Sir Denys Lasdun enters his 80th year and the Hallfield School prepares for its 40th anniversary, it is thought provoking to reflect on a time after the war when these circumstances wouldn't have been 'exceptional'.

Katherine MacInnes

Notes

1 *News Chronicle,* 3.9.54.

2 Ibid.

3 Andrew Saint, *Towards a Social Architecture – The Role of School Building in Post-War England,* Yale University Press.

4 Stuart Maclure, *Educational development and school building: aspects of public policy 1945-1973,* Longman.

5 *West London Chronicle,* September 1954.

6 *Architectural Design,* interview 30.6.94.

7 Denys Lasdun, *Architecture, City and Landscape,* Phaidon, 1994.

8 *News Chronicle,* 3.9.54.

9 *Architectural Design,* interview, 30.6.94.

10 *THE ARCHITECT and Building news,* 17.11. 55.

11 *Evening Standard,* 24.6.94.

References: *Architectural Design* 1961 June and Feb; *Architectural Review* 1955 Sept; *Architects' Journal* 1955 March

Single storey Infant School in the foreground, double storey administration department with staff room patio in the background
Photographs (colour): Mario Bettella

IN FINITE STATE MACHINES

LIVING MACHINES
Ted Kruger

The development of computation machinery in the last half of the 20th century is one of the primary developments during this period. Shrinking from room-size constructions to desktop units to hand-held devices – they are posed to disappear into the woodwork. This migration fundamentally changes the nature of the environments that we inhabit. The walls themselves are becoming intelligent.

While this is not yet obvious in the field of architecture, it is evident in many other objects of everyday use. The cost of electronics in the average automobile now exceeds the cost of the steel[1] and there appears to be an imbedded processor in every appliance. As well, there are efforts to facilitate the communication between these objects that could take place within architectural environments.[2] This development comes about because of an ideology of facilitation. Individual decisions are made on the basis of the increasing functionality that the implementation allows. The results of these many simple and independent decisions will be both complex and profound.

I would argue that the greatest influence of computers in architecture will not come from CAD or other visualisation tools, but from the distribution of intelligence into the fabric of the buildings and the objects contained within. We must question what role architecture is to play within the context of intelligent environments.

This process has been started in buildings. An interesting proposal has been outlined by Smith, Takeuchi and Shah at Stanford University[3] where not only would buildings be fitted out to send and react to seismic waves, but to send early warning information to other buildings on its network. Structures close to the epicentre may only have time to react in a limited way, but remote buildings would be able to take more complex actions. Not only will the buildings have sensors and actuators, but the structures will be able to communicate with each other.

One can consider an aggregation of communicating machines to be an instance of cellular automata. These logical constructs were proposed by Von Neumann in an effort to understand the workings of both natural systems and computers. Cellular automata are collections of finite state machines typically arrayed in a uniform lattice. Each cell determines its state based upon simple rules relating its current state to the state of the adjacent cells. Those familiar with Conway's 'Game of Life' will recognise that complex behaviours can be derived from sets of simple rules. It has been shown that all the logical elements for computation can spontaneously arise within this CA.

Recent work by Langton[4] indicates that in cellular automata the emergence of complex dynamics involving information processing occurs at a critical phase transition between ordered and disordered states. Langton speculates that life itself occurs in the vicinity of this phase transition.

One can conclude that complex behaviours will emerge from the interactions inherent within intelligent environments. It is not possible to determine from the outset what their nature will be. The work shown here takes the position that lifelike behaviours are not only a possibility but of sufficient probability to merit investigation. The work consists of two rectangular boxes from which project 24 tapering rods. One's presence between the boxes triggers an adjacent rod into a slow graceful bend. The motion is fluid and completely silent. Others soon follow, arching forward or to one side and then the other. After you move on, the activity continues and it becomes clear that the rods were not reacting to you, but that the reaction of the initial rod was spreading through the population in a series of ripples – that the rods are reacting to each other. The intent is to create a work that is simultaneously machine, plant and social insect. Each of the rods are tensed by two fine strands of Shape Memory Alloy (SMA) wire. SMAs are a class of alloys that exhibit an unusual effect due to differences in the crystalline structure of their martensitic and austenitic phases. When cool, the metal is easily deformed, but when heated above the transition temperature to the austente phase it recovers its original shape and in the process is capable of work.[5] The wire used in this project is fabricated from a nickel/titanium alloy marketed under the trade name Flexinol. It is 150 um in diameter and has a deformation force of 62g and produces approximately 330g of recovery force.[6] Each strand of SMA wire is 1.5 M long and recovers approximately 60mm when resistance heated with 24 VDC.

While current research is concerned with

FROM ABOVE: Installation at Katonah Museum, Katonah, New York: Interior of base computer; Tapered rods.

increasing the reaction time of the alloy for use as robotic actuators,[7] in this case, the wire length was chosen beyond the suppliers' specifications to decrease the response rate for aesthetic effect. This had additional benefits. As there was no danger of overheating, the temperature of the wire did not have to be monitored. A steamlining of the sensing and control functions resulted. In addition, because the mass of the SMA strand is very small, the reaction becomes sensitive to ambient temperature and wind conditions. The work responds more quickly and strongly in hot weather, while in winter it will not react at all.[8]

The tapered rods are fabricated from a graphite/epoxy composite[9] and provide sufficient bias force to stretch the SMA in its low temperature state. The hollow rods serve as a conduit for wiring that supplies power and ground connections to the SMA wires that are fastened to the black acrylic brackets secured to the rods. The lower bracket holds the wires out away from the axis of the rod and provides a reverse bias mechanism[10] as the alloy contracts and the rod is loaded eccentrically. The two wires provide four possible states for each rod. Each rod constitutes a finite state machine implemented in hardware and assumes a position based on the state of the surrounding rods or the switches in a manner similar to cellular automata. No attempt has been made to programme the activity of the rods as a group but relationships between them are established and the group's activity emerges from the individual interactions.

In software, each SMA wire is controlled by a variable. The value of this variable is determined by simple rules that reference the state of 'adjacent' variables to compute its new state. Adjacency is specified relative to the irregular spatial distribution of the rods rather than by reference to a uniform lattice. The states are computed and then implemented in discrete time steps.

Each base contains a computer that was assembled from modular input, output and processor cards in a proprietary backplane.[11] The processor is an 8-bit Intel 8052 AH. Programming was done Basic. The code was converted to C and implemented with a corresponding graphics display running on a Silicon Graphics work station to verify the sequences[12] while the project was under construction. The bases are simple plywood boxes that are covered in a resin/aluminium powder product that is used for the repair of boat hulls. This material was ground smooth and waxed to give the bases a metallic monolithic quality.[13]

The work undertaken here draws on research done in preparation for a seminar in technology transfer given by the author at the Graduate School of Architecture, Planning and Preservation at Columbia University. This course looks at technologies that are available or developing in non-architectural fields that have potential applications within architecture. Among the areas considered are intelligent materials and structures, robotics, complexity studies and computation. The underlying thesis is that the importation of these technologies into architecture can fundamentally change the definition of the architectural problem. The task may be redefined as the creation of environments that are casually indistinguishable from biological systems. The current project is an initial exploration of what those environments will become.

Ted Krueger is the principal of 'Living Machines', a research organisation dedicated to exploiting technologies with the objective of building intelligent synthetic organisms.

Installation at Katonah Museum, Katonah, New York: A series of images showing movement of tapered rods.

Notes

1 Forbes study cited in *Wired* 2.06, p 26, June 94.

2 K Davidson, 'Habitech 94', *Computer Applications Journal* # 47, p46, June 94.

3 H A Smith Y Takeuchi & H Shah, 'An Advance Notification System for Smart Structures in Seismic Zones', 1st European Conference on Smart Structures and Materials, *SPIE* Vol 1777, 1992.

4 C Langton 'Life at the Edge of Chaos' in *Artificial Life II*, Proceedings Vol X, Santa Fe Institute Studies in the Science of Complexity, Addison-Wesley, Redwood City, CA 1992.

5 R Gilbertson, *Working with Shape Memory Wires*, Mondotronics, Inc, 1991.

6 Mondotronics Product Literature, undated.

7 K Kuribayshi 'Improvement of the response of an SMA Actucator using a Temperature Sensor', *The International Journal of Robotics Research* Vol 10, No 1 Feb 1991.

8 The work was commissioned by the Katonah Museum in Westchester County, New York for the exhibition 'Shelter and Dreams' curated by Jane Dodds. The exhibition, in an outdoor sculpture garden starts on April 22, 1994 and remains in place until November 13. The expected temperature variation during this period was one of the design considerations.

9 These were purchased off-the-shelf from a fishing rod manufacturer.

10 Gilbertson.

11 Alpha Products, Inc A-Bus System.

12 Lyle Seuss, a graduate student at the GSAPP, Columbia University was responsible for the simulation. Additional programming assistance was provided by Paul Krueger.

13 Much of the construction and assembly was undertaken by Bill Massie of Sub Urban Building Studio of New York assisted by Corey Saft and Scott Enge. Jean Krueger provided assistance and support over the duration of the project.

A WALL THAT.. . . . . . .

MATTHEW BARNETT HOWLAND

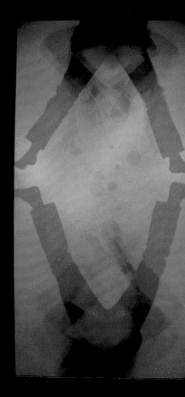

A shape slopes into the room. It looks like Kate, and as she turns, the size of the ears confirm this. She's not feeling good this morning – you can tell by the way she moves. The wall can't decide how to respond immediately, and remains inactive while it ponders. It's had a bad dream in the night, and is still slightly dazed.

The human eye allows information about the world to enter the body. The patterns of light that converge on the retina of the eye are recorded chemically, producing short-lived phosphorescent after-images. The connectivity of the massive network of neurons in the brain allow it to think about what its sensory organs, such as the eyes, are gathering. It can remember what it has seen, relate this to what it is seeing, learn from this process, and then dream about these visual experiences. The structure of this organic neural net is the basis for a computerised model of the brain that is being studied in the realm of Artificial Intelligence. Mechanical analogues of the human visual processing system have already been developed – from memory, to the capacity for learning and even dreaming about what has been seen.

It is in this context that a piece of architectural fabric, such as a wall, has the potential to develop a genuine mechanical analogue of human 'intelligence'. A wall that receives and records visual information about the space it defines is a wall that sees. A wall that can assimilate this information into its existing understanding of the world is also a wall that learns. When input is turned off, this artificial neural network wanders around its memory firing randomly, 'dreaming'. Therefore, the wall is the eye of an architecture that can think and dream about its occupation.

At a practical level, a wall covered in photo-luminescent paint has a kind of material intelligence in that it can remember light. Using a light source to cast a shadow of someone onto the wall, an image of the spatial relationship between the three can be retained in the depth of the wall itself. This is not a camera image, but an *image of presence*, created by the interaction of people and light in the space in front of the wall. The physicality of this image is important in view of the idea that intelligence is in some way curiously physical in its origins. The wall is

already starting to see and remember information about the world it sits in. For example, each position in plan has a unique silhouette in elevation, allowing patterns of movement to be mapped spatially. Other information about the person can be deduced from the way they move, their gestures and facial expressions. To allow for more genuinely intelligent characteristics to develop, however, this kind of information would have to be processed by an artificial neural net. An electronic version of the wall enables this kind of computerised element to be incorporated. The manner in which the essentially spatial image is formed remains the same, but the means by which the wall sees and records this image involves the use of video technology. The wall is made of a translucent material, so that the silhouette can be seen from both sides. This image is filmed, and replayed in negative by a video projector back onto the wall. The image is also replayed on a brief strobo-scopic delay, to achieve the effect of the wall remembering the image of you in different positions in the space. This information about the different ways in which the space is occupied over time is then processed by an artificially intelligent computer. In the practical project, this is achieved using the audio-visual capabilities of a Macintosh to embody the principle of interaction that is central to the idea of an architecture that can receive, think about and then respond to information about the world.

Ideally the wall itself would be an artificial neural net comprising billions of interconnected cells, able to learn and evolve as it spent more time taking part in the world. The manner in which rooms, buildings and whole streets might respond more actively depends upon the mental picture of the world that they are able to construct.

In as much as architecture is the design of things that sit in the world, this conceptual model of intelligence that is centred upon experience of a physical environment suggests an immediate relevance to the field of 'intelligent' building. 'Responsive' and 'intelligent' environments as they stand are usually controlled by conventionally programmed systems, whereas the kind of intelligence that is generated by artificial neural networks has greater flexibility and therefore far greater potential.

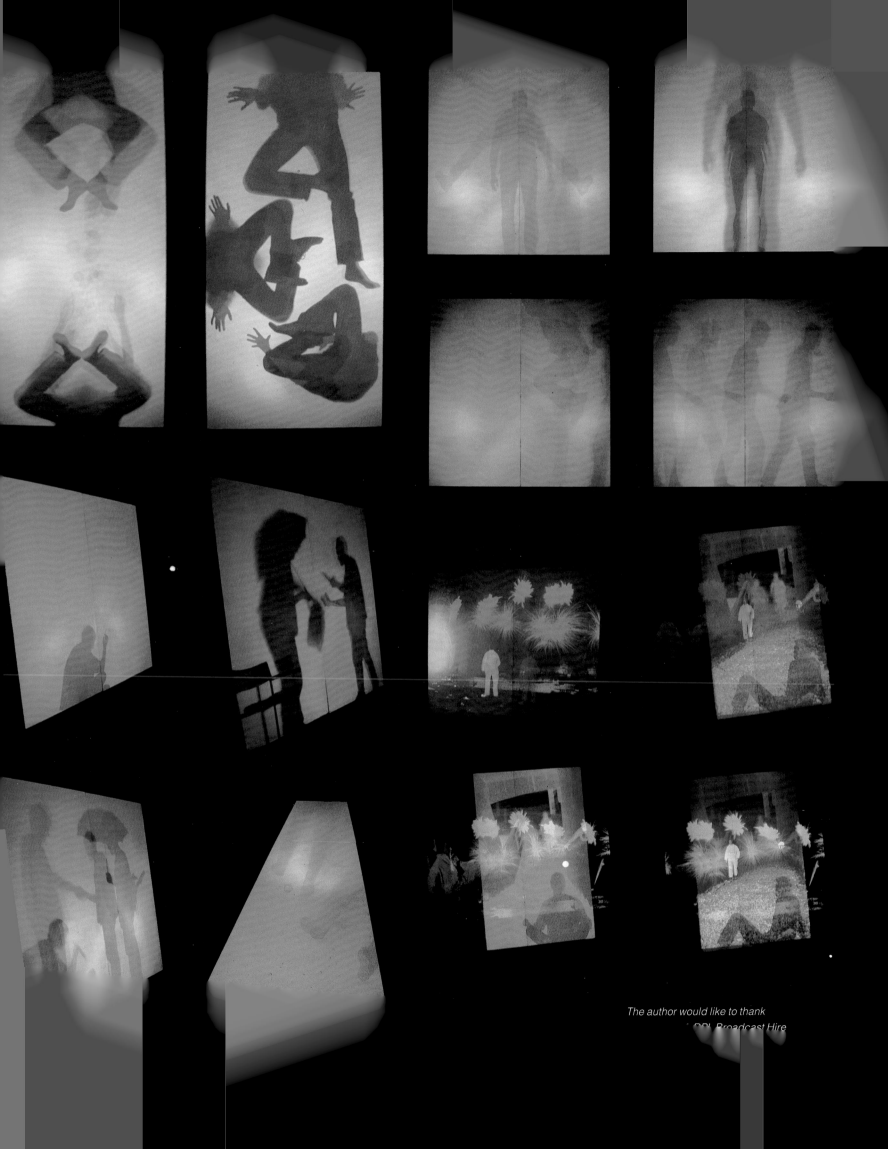

The author would like to thank
DPL Broadcast Hire

THE ARCHITECTURE OF INCARCERATION

A wealth of new correctional facilities has been built around the globe but there appears to be a lack of published analytical evaluation in response to this type of architecture. This volume brings together USA and European 20th-century developments and provides an international focus on the complex architecture of confinement, featuring a selection of incisive texts and strong colour images of built, projected and conceptual schemes. This book affords a unique insight into buildings that are tailored to a very specific and unusual brief. The text includes a foreword by HM Inspector of Prisons, Judge Tumin and major essays by Leslie Fairweather and Professor Thomas A Markus among others.

HB ISBN: 1 85490 358 6   £35
305x252mm, 128 pages
Extensively illustrated in colour and black and white
September 1994

DESIGNING THE FUTURE OF THE SOUTH BANK

T he role of the cultural centre in the 21st century is an issue which has implications throughout the world. The South Bank as the most powerful concentration of arts resources in the UK is, and has been for a number of years, the focus of international debate. Collaboration between the Academy Group and the South Bank Centre resulted in a symposium earlier this year in which the future of the site was discussed. A broad range of professionals gave their personal interpretation of the issue and the discussion swung between those defending the existing structure and those who suggested that several features should be redesigned from scratch. The Academy book will be published in conjunction with an exhibition held at the South Bank itself when the winner of the competition will be announced. The publication will present the ten short listed schemes along with the three finalists. It will also feature highlights of the proceedings at the symposium.

PB ISBN: 1 85490 403 5   £15.95
279x217mm 96 pages
Black and while and colour illustrations throughout
September 1994

ARCHITECTURE & FILM

*A*rchitectural Design will explore ideas about the interaction of film and architecture in the next issue. This exciting new area of debate allows us to develop an original perspective on the issues surrounding the similarities between two seemingly contrasting methods of creating. Filmmaker, Jan Vrijman, supervised the first Film and Architecture workshop at the Berlage Institute in Amsterdam which reached the conclusion that there were more similarities than differences: 'A storyboard is a filmmakers equivalent to the architect's drawing: a representational means towards an end. Action in film is usually highly contrived and artificial yet once life inhabits the direction architecture gives it, it takes on a form of its own, an 'improvisation' sometimes differing from design intentions.' In America, the Architecture on Screen festival organised by The Metropolitan Museum of Art and the J Paul Getty Trust suggested that 'Architecture has a natural affinity for the moving image. Time, space and motion are the basis of both art forms and film/video can transport views to architectural sites all over the world.'

Architectural Design Issue No 112
AD Vol 64, No 11-12/1994
Price £14.95
October 1994

CHARLES RENNIE MACKINTOSH,
Synthesis in Form
by James Steele

*T*he recent RIBA exhibition CR Mackintosh: 'The Chelsea Years 1915-23', concentrates on the time that Mackintosh spent in London. The show concentrates on many of his unrealised architectural projects, including the dramatic remodelling of 78 Derngate, Northampton. In the Academy publication, James Steele traces Mackintosh's work from his early days as an apprentice in Glasgow through to the late 1920s spent in Provence. A unique insight into the man is achieved through a detailed analysis of his work as a painter between 1914-15 and the effect that this had on his subsequent return to architecture. An in-depth analysis of the Glasgow School of Art, the Glasgow Herald Building, the Daily Record Building, Martyr's Public School, Queen's Cross Church, Queen Margaret's Medical College, the Tea Rooms, Windyhill and the Hill House is followed by comparing Mackintosh's work with his contemporary architects: MacLaren, Voysey and Baillie-Scott.

HB ISBN 1 85490 383 7   Price £45
305 x 252mm, 256 pages
Fully illustrated throughout
October 1994

Further information can be obtained from Academy Group Ltd 071 402 2141

SWEET DISORDER AND THE CAREFULLY CARELESS Theory and Criticism in Architecture by Robert Maxwell, Princeton Papers on Architecture, Princeton University Press, 330pp, PB £N/A

Not a word is wasted – in contrast to much contemporary criticism this collection of Maxwell's short essays provides a powerful insight to the rich symbiosis of criticism and theory. Maxwell exhibits a rare precision of beautifully constructed and surgically precise arguments which are the necessary result of the condensed magazine format from which the works are, with some editing, drawn. This is a book of balance, an attempt to explain the horror vacuum of the late 20th century which is a product of the dialectic struggle between science and art. In both theory and criticism he attempts to capture at a moment that which makes the eternal philosophical paradox tangible: male and female, love and hate, past and future. Despite the eternal state of flux there are moments of clarity. For Hereclitus, as for Maxwell and Schopenhauer, the contemplation of a work of art provides solace from this unbearable dichotomy.

For Maxwell the work of Francis Bacon most powerfully brings this moment to appearance. The polarities of despair and exhilaration, figuration and abstraction, past and future, are presented to the observer instantaneously juxtaposed yet unresolved, like a flash of lightning into the soul. In architecture James Stirling captures the same moment of insight. Here carefully controlled oppositions within the same building, most notably the Braun Pharmaceutical Headquarters, Melsungen, Germany, lie unresolved but so carefully juxtaposed to at once provide the necessary doubt of reason and the humanity of belief and in this we find a chink of light illuminating the underlying dilemma of existence. Maxwell's position is both a heartfelt lament for, and defence of the otherwise unspoken ideology of Sir James Stirling, and hence the book is dedicated to Stirling: 'a good friend and a true architect'.

In Stirling's work he finds the substance for an architectural philosophy of the 'both/and', whilst Venturi is relegated to the pastiche of appliqué and ornamentation despite its supposed deep structure of complexity and contradiction. Maxwell is at his best in exploring the ideological nuances of these icons of Post-Modern architecture and his comparison of their respective entries for the National Gallery competition, London. 'The existence of each one calls out for the other to restore a balance in the field. This is the reason why at a lower level, conducts such as those evoked by sweet disorder and the carefully careless have merit; they are positions taken on the tightrope and are aware of the two extremes'.

This is moreover the optimism of the latter combined with the pessimism of the former and here he treads that very same tightrope in a precarious fact value equation. Strangely the tradition of the English landscape most completely expresses the carefully careless since in its inevitable contrivance it subjects us to the force of entropy. Sweet disorder becomes something less tangible equating to Maxwell's experience as Dean at Princeton over the last 12 years in the liberated expression manifest in the Americana of free form architecture. Herein perhaps lies the essence of his work in an attempt to achieve a balance, or at least simultaneous moment to explain both.
Martin Pearce

ROBERT ADAM Drawings and Imagination by AA Tait, Cambridge University Press, 174pp, 153 ills, HB £N/A

This book, meant primarily for academics of architecture, focuses on the 18th-century architect Robert Adam and his pen, wash and watercolour 'inventions'; picturesque inventions, of which, over a thousand have survived. The years following 1773 showed a waning of the 'internationalism' and the growth of the fashionable style of the picturesque where building was an integral component of scenery. Rather than the conventional tools and techniques of architecture, Adam interprets colour and movement, looking beyond pure draughtsmanship to the variety and mood of the design that existed in the mind. *The Works* signalled a way forward, a *tour de force*, with an indivisible bond between drawing, building and planting: break away from a classicism of precise and restrictive categories.

GLYNDEBOURNE Building a Vision by Marcus Binney and Rosy Runciman, Thames and Hudson, 1994, 160pp, b/w and col ills, HB £16.95

In conjunction with the opening of the new Opera House, this publication encompasses the history of Glyndebourne, both past and present, with historical material and plans and photographs of the present work. Subdivided into three main sections: a personal introduction by Sir George Christie; the history of the house by Rosy Runciman; and Glyndebourne in the late 80s by Marcus Binney, it highlights that the result is 'not just a triumph, but a great masterpiece'. The new 'eclipsical' Opera House incorporates the circular geometry of the auditorium, staircases, foyers and back-stage areas, in a design of great simplicity and consistency, and still with the spirit of the old Glyndebourne.

URBAN DESIGN The American Experience by Jon Lang, International Thomson Publishing, 1994, 509pp, b/w ills, HB £43.00

Urban design in the USA is analysed through psychology in this publication. By applying this empirical humanism, Jon Lang develops a forum for questions about design and society as a whole. In the USA, urban design had a strong pragmatic orientation, with its roots in the modern movement (Rationalism and Empiricism) in architecture, in particular the failures of the movement to recognise human experience and urban life, especially after World War II urban expansion and social policies. It became a commodity, profitable, market-oriented. Divided into four sections, this book observes urban design, designer/architect issues and empirical knowledge, what is meant by 'empiricism', and the distinction between urban design as a discipline and as a professional activity if not a profession. In general, this consumer-based design should give way to the social obligations of the designer and public interest requirements.

THE NEW CITY The American City edited by Jean-François Lejeune, Princeton Architectural Press, 1994, 151pp, b/w and col ills, HB £N/A

Centred around four essays and four projects, this book traces the urban environment from Jeffersonian concepts in Virginia to 'visual simulations' of the States of New York, New Jersey

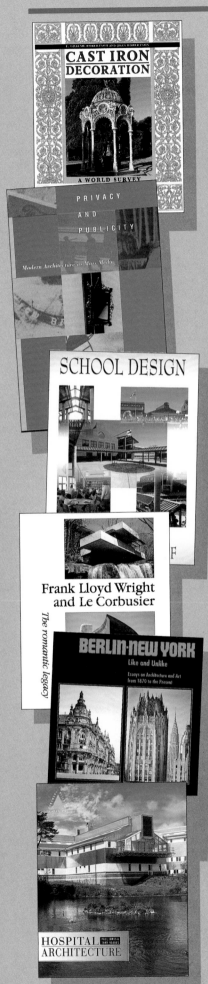

and Connecticut. Position has replaced expansion with an emphasis on a grid-landscape relationship, a city-region interconnection, urban spaces and nature, and monumentality in architecture. Based on this Jeffersonian ideology of public buildings and a political centre providing happiness and pleasure within the urban environment, the book gradually unfolds the hierarchical and topological structure of The American City. This is achieved through the courthouse, the courthouse square, the campus as a town within a city, the aesthetic and visual character as well as the physical planning of the city.

CAST IRON DECORATION A World Survey by E Graeme Robertson and Joan Robertson, Thames and Hudson, 1994, 336pp, b/w ills, HB £19.95
Cast iron decoration plays a subservient role to architecture. It rarely seems to rise to the status of a great independent work, despite an amazing variety of forms and a richness of design. However, through a worldwide survey backed with historical research of iron production and iron work, the authors highlight the ornamental variations between countries, the relationship cast iron decoration has with architecture and hence its aestheticism. From the British Isles to Australia, the global cultural heritage is conveyed. This once 'subservient' artform, through detailed descriptions and an abundance of illustrations, becomes a scholarly entity.

PRIVACY AND PUBLICITY Modern Architecture as Mass Media by Beatriz Colomina, The MIT Press, 1994, 389pp, b/w ills, HB £34.95
Space and subjectivity are displaced as architecture becomes engaged with the mass media. The ideology of modern architecture is questioned and architectural criticism is reconsidered. The author believes that modern architecture was produced through emerging systems of communication and not as a high artistic practice in opposition to mass culture, as conventional criticism portrays. Architecture is viewed in a different way, by the use of film, photographs, drawings, but at all times the piece of architecture is never abandoned. It is viewed as a mechanism of representation in its own right. Space alters as architecture renegotiates the traditional relationship between public and private. '. . . the peripheral turns out to be the central.'

SCHOOL DESIGN by Henry Sanoff, Van Nostrand Reinhold, 1994, 215pp, b/w ills, HB £49.50
A lack of user participation has been cited as a major reason for dissatisfaction. Yet these same users are a valuable source for the ways buildings should look and be developed. Shaping the learning environment to support educational objectives is one of the central themes of this book, a process that involves teachers, students, parents, administrators and architects. Despite tight monetary budgets, it is seen that even minor design modifications can have a major positive effect on the school performance. '...design can change students' behaviour, increase interaction with materials, decrease interruptions, promote more substantive questioning and ultimately improve academic achievement.' After all, the school environment should encourage dialogue, debate and collaboration. Therefore, participation, as a direct human involvement, is important for decision-making processes. The result is a social, democratic, didactic effect with a higher intellectual level of school community.

FRANK LLOYD WRIGHT AND LE CORBUSIER The Romantic Legacy by Richard A Etlin, Manchester University Press, 1994, 222pp, b/w and col ills, HB £25.00
The highly original and controversial architecture Frank Lloyd Wright and Le Corbusier has had a profound influence on 20th-century architecture world wide. Richard A Etlin offers new insights into formative influences of the time to provide a context from which to analyse the extent to which work of these great architects was unique.

To provide a background, he analyses the architectural theories of the time such as 'the architectural system', 'the picturesque', 'philosophical eclecticism' and the 'spirit of the age'. By exploring the various ways in which each architect chose to approach these principles he attempts to demonstrate that an adherence to these values was 'the surest way to create new and timeless works that their fellows and future generations would recognise as worthy testimonies to the age'.

BERLIN-NEW YORK Like and Unlike: Essays on Architecture and Art from 1870 to the Present edited by Josef Paul Kleihues and Christina

Rathgeber, Rizzoli, 1994, 511pp, b/w ills, HB £65.00
Berlin-New York identifies parallels and contrasts between the two great world metropolises of the late 19th century, cities which have developed dramatically during the 'Second Industrial Revolution'. Society at this time saw rapid developments in technology and especially in new building materials for new building types. The result is an ever-changing New York and a Berlin which is in a process of rebuilding.

Divided into three historical sections, 1870-1918, 1918-1945 and 1945-present, the book addresses the questions of urban planning – transportation networks, the skyscraper, the garden city movement, inner city housing and the modern movement.

Although this book is a collection of in-depth essays highlighting the problems and opportunities confronting New York and Berlin, the past couple of years have seen great debate over the restructuring and rebuilding of Berlin, issues which have not been covered within the 'present' section.

Contributors include architects and critics Peter Blake, Herbert Muschamp, Kenneth Frampton, Vittorio M Lampugnani, Robert AM Stern and art historians Dore Ashton, Patricia Hills and Wieland Schmied.

HOSPITAL ARCHITECTURE by Paul James and Tony Noakes, Longman , 1994, 168pp, b/w and col ills, HB £60.00
Medicine is an ever-changing field which demands new and better working environments, for the benefit of the patients. From a global survey, Hospital Architecture emphasises the quality of the facilities provided for both staff and patients and questions whether 'hospitals can be architecture'. Based on a study of 28 hospitals, ranging from community units to large teaching institutions, the authors address the issues of aesthetics and challenge whether they are acceptable. From a social point of view, the relationship between patients and staff, and how this can affect the hospital, patients etc is also covered. With the upgrading of existing hospitals rather than building new ones (because of a severe reduction in finance), hospitals need to assess the functional suitability and maintenance costs of the health care environment.

reviews *books*

SHIN TAKAMATSU edited by Paolo Polledri, San Francisco Museum of Modern Art and Rizzoli, 1993, 139pp, b/w and col ills, PB £N/A

Shin Takamatsu's architecture exemplifies a distinctively Japanese movement in which a synthesis of traditional forms, post-structuralist theories and high individualistic visions is displacing the Western rationalist and modernist impulses of preceding generations. Whenever he becomes identified by a building, confined to a particular manner, or is left open to interpretation he startles his critics with a change in direction and approach; each project questions the previous work. The result is a collection of buildings which are practical, functional and critical of the current Japanese urban environment. While they seem to be fuelled, even contaminated, by the external, restless world, they seem to become compositional systems that stand alone. An 'isolation' where the interaction of theory and design are strongly exemplified. If Takamatsu's work ethic is an accurate indication of future developments, he promises extraordinary new work.

FROM SOUTHGATE TO HALLWOOD PARK – 25 Years in the life of a Runcorn Community by Jane Morton, Merseyside Improved Houses, 1994, 140pp, b/w and col ills, PB £10.99

In December 1968, Runcorn Development Corporation approved plans for an estate to house some 6,000 people at Southgate on a site beside the new shopping centre then being built for Runcorn. It was thought that the scheme 'could very well set a new standard in housing design in this country.' Just over 20 years later in February 1989, Warrington and Runcorn Development Corporation approved the demolition of Southgate.

In this well illustrated study, Jane Morton examines how the responsibility of housing a single community over 25 years was handled and considers what lessons can be learnt for the future. She traces the construction and subsequent management of Southgate; the search for solutions that ended in the decision to demolish; the vigorous campaign mounted by Southgate Residents Association and Merseyside Improved Houses to fight for new homes on the same site; and the complicated demolition, decanting and construction project which became the prestigious and award winning Hallwood Park.

GWATHMEY SIEGEL Buildings and Projects 1982-1992, Rizzoli, 1993, 336pp, b/w and col ills, £N/A

This well illustrated book conveys a decade of buildings and projects in which European modernism and New England puritanism are combined into a pragmatic formalism. A formalism in which conceptual mechanisms highlight a formal ordering, ie hollowing, rotation, extension and movement within the building. No matter what the project, the end result never seems to challenge this institutional frame. All areas of practice are covered, namely educational/arts buildings, corporate buildings, building interiors and residential buildings, with a collective section on buildings, projects, furniture and objects. The firm, to much acclaim, recently finished a complete restoration of and major addition to Frank Lloyd Wright's Guggenheim Museum in New York. The work ethic for this project was not only to save the original, but, from an archaeological discovery, to enrich the spatial experience while maintaining Wright's vision of architectural integrity.

THE COMPLETE LANDSCAPE DESIGNS AND GARDENS OF GEOFFREY JELLICOE by Michael Spens, Thames and Hudson, 1994, 212pp, 243 ills, 108 in colour, HB £36.00

Urban and rural life is now shaped by ecological considerations which even a decade ago were considered to be peripheral. The divisions that existed between architecture and landscape have been removed. Geoffrey Jellicoe has helped with this transformation. Project by project, this authoritative monograph examines his works through his 'early works', 'a philosophy of landscape and garden design' and 'full flowering: the master period from 1980'. Several schemes have been photographed to depict the development of the work, notable Ditchley, St Paul's Walden Bury and Shute. His work fits truly within the Modernist concept, yet retains the measure of historical understanding, in particular Italian Renaissance humanism, and links design to philosophy to label him as a Classicist-Modernist. Throughout the book are original drawings, of which Jellicoe says, 'the truth of my ideas is *only* in the drawings'. The inclusion of the author's words and drawings and beautiful photographs make this monograph a valuable resource for anyone interested in landscape designs and gardens.

RICHARD HENRIQUEZ: Memory Theatre edited by Howard Shubert, MIT Press, 1994, 81pp, b/w and col ills, PB £14.25

Working within the constraints of typical commercial commissions, Richard Henriquez is making a very untypical contribution, both to the quality of the built environment in and around Vancouver and to the symbolic lexicon of architecture in general. He engages his buildings in a dialogue between architecture and ecological and native history. This monograph provides insight into the architect's strategies and uncovers his personal origins that drive his process of design. And through this personal vision he gives us poetic work that belongs to the most authentic historical tradition of architecture as a form of knowledge, an architecture that transcends the outdated classicism of the 19th century. The Memory Theatre defines a 'place in the world' based on the memory of events, persons, past experiences, and the 'inner depths of the human soul, in this case the architect's own'.

EAMES HOUSE by Marilyn Neuhart and John Neuhart, Ernst & Sohn, 1994, 64pp, b/w and col ills, HB £N/A

The Eames House, 1949, designed for and by Charles and Ray Eames became a pivotal structure in the history of 20th-century architecture. It became an exhibition unto itself, a microcosm and an encapsulation of the designers' lives.

This elegant English-German publication highlights the personal lifestyles of the Eames, their connection with *Arts & Architecture* (a magazine dedicated to the Modern Movement) and how it was to become the symbol of the 'Case Study House Program'. The house stands as 'a metaphor for off-the-shelf, prefabricated industrial construction translated to residential building'. Likened to a Mondrian painting that was anything but anonymous, the Eames House transcends the combination of steel, stucco and glass. While the exercise to design and build a personal home is irreverent, playful and yet earnest, it speaks of true 'work'. It remains an eloquent example of modern architecture and lays the groundwork for architecture yet to be built.

RICHARD MEIER Building for Art
edited by Werner Blaser, Birkhäuser Verlag, 1994, 179pp, b/w ills, HB £N/A
With texts by Richard Meier, John Walsh, Director of the J Paul Getty Museum, Los Angeles, Gudmund Vigtel, Director of The High Museum of Art, Atlanta, and Werner Blaser, this book traces the requirements for museum architecture construction. External and internal space, lighting, the visitor and the artwork and the way in which all of these interact with the museum building itself are clearly discussed – the museum building becomes more than a 'mere backdrop to the displays of art'. Richard Meier's architectural principles and personal philosophy are interspersed among project descriptions and linked to Vitruvian principles. This present day interpretation particularly points to the significance of 'appropriateness and usefulness (utilitas), strength and durability (firmitas) and beauty of proportion and scale (venustas)'. Works include The New York School Exhibition, The Museum of Modern Art at the Villa Strozzi, Museum für Kunsthandwerk, The High Museum of Art, the Des Moines Art Center Addition and the J Paul Getty Center.

DELAYED SPACE Work of Homa Fardjadi and Mohsen Mostafavi edited by Julia Collins, Princeton Architectural Press, 1994, 147pp, b/w and col ills, £N/A
This monograph presents recent work by architects Homa Fardjadi and Mohsen Mostafavi. The current trend in both architectural practice and criticism towards extremities in theory has in some circles ruled out a discussion of actual buildings. Excluded from such discourse is the 'middle ground' of architecture – the space of the building itself. The work of Homa Fardjadi and Mohsen Mostafavi forces a reconsideration of this middle ground as more than the site of daily functioning, but as 'that which instigates the activities it also contains and presents'. The elements of personal engagement, production of effects, events and actions 'promise to overcome one of the major failures of modern architecture: being something for everyone but for no one in particular.'

BUSSTOPS International Design Project Hannover edited by Lothar Romain, Verlag Th Schäfer, 1994, 223pp, b/w and col ills, HB DM 79
The international design project

BUSSTOPS leaves the sphere of pure functional design conquering public space. Representing the creative limits achievable between art, sculpture and architecture, Andreas Brandolini, Frank O Gehry, Massimo Iosa Ghini, Wolfgang Laubersheimer, Alessandro Mendini, Jasper Morrison, Heike Mühlhaus, Ettore Sottsass and Oscar Tusquets have designed nine bus- and tramstops for Hannover. With comprehensive articles, illustrations and photographs this German-English book follows the embryonic architectural stages, with initial conceptions and sketches, through to the finished constructions set within the urban environment. 'There is nothing like Hannover's BUSSTOPS anywhere in the world. They are a pioneering step taken by the artists who designed them, opening up new areas to art.' The BUSSTOPS have moved from the model stage into real life, with a confident expressiveness, unfolding their unique qualities and extending beyond their function.

PARK GÜELL by Conrad Kent and Dennis Prindle, Princeton Architectural Press, 1993, 223pp, b/w and col ills, PB £N/A
The ingenuity of Park Güell, among the urban environment of Barcelona, has resulted from an opposition to functionalist engineering and secular social sciences. Enthused by religion and culture the result is a colourful ceramic and stone maze, which was 'a programme for reconnecting a people to the fundamental realities of their land and culture'. The desire was to create a unique community different from the outside world, yet a community which is in strict engagement with that world – a garden of delights. The image of paradise, analogous to the religiously based regionalist culture, was seen as the idyllic solution to the human condition. Today, one can still ponder the maze of colour that reconnected a residential community. This thoroughly researched book is complemented by both archival and contemporary photographs, measured drawings and a selection of colour plates.

BENTHEM CROUWEL by Vincent van Rossem, Uitgeverij 010, 1994, 144pp, b/w ills, HB Fl 59.50
This book sets out to document in a surveyable form the work of the Dutch architects Jan Bentham and Mels Crouwel. The architects are still young, and with a changing Europe

both financially and technologically will continue to expand the stimulating series of houses they have built. Jan Benthem's house, a glass box resting on a space frame, was immediately on completion the subject of great international attention. This transparent architecture typifies the later projects too, such as the customs stations at Hazeldonk and Oldenzaal, the extensions to Amsterdam Airport and the recent additions to the Anne Frank Museum – a few examples taken from the 18th-century projects described in this book. Part of a series, this book appears at the instigation of the Prins Bernhard Fonds under the auspices of the Dutch Architectural Institute.

RESEALING OF BUILDING A Guide to Good Practice by Ron Woolman, Butterworth Heineman, 1994, 169pp, b/w ills, PB £25.00
This guide is a result of the DOE/EPSRC LINK Construction Maintenance and Refurbishment Programme, a major UK Government initiative to promote academic and industrial collaboration to tackle fundamental problems in the construction industry. It is based on the findings of the RESEAL project, which ran from 1989 to 1992, managed by a team consisting of Oxford Brookes University, Taywood Engineering Limited and a sealant manufacturers' consortium. A substantial proportion of the cost of building maintenance is attributable to resealing of the external envelope, a task which is significantly more difficult than sealant installation during new build. In 1990, approximately 100,00km of building joints were resealed in the UK at a total cost in excess of £500m. This is a comprehensive and practical guide to good construction and resealing practice embodying a concentration on the entire period, from its inception in the early 1950s to the present day.

The reference to the M16 Building by Terry Farrell in the article 'Is Intelligent the Opposite of Clever?' by Katherine MacInnes (March/April issue of Architectural Design) implies that the user was forced to adapt the building from the architect's initial concept design. We understand that this is in fact not the case. The clients are entirely happy with the work of Terry Farrell and they have said that the purpose designed building is well tailored to their needs.

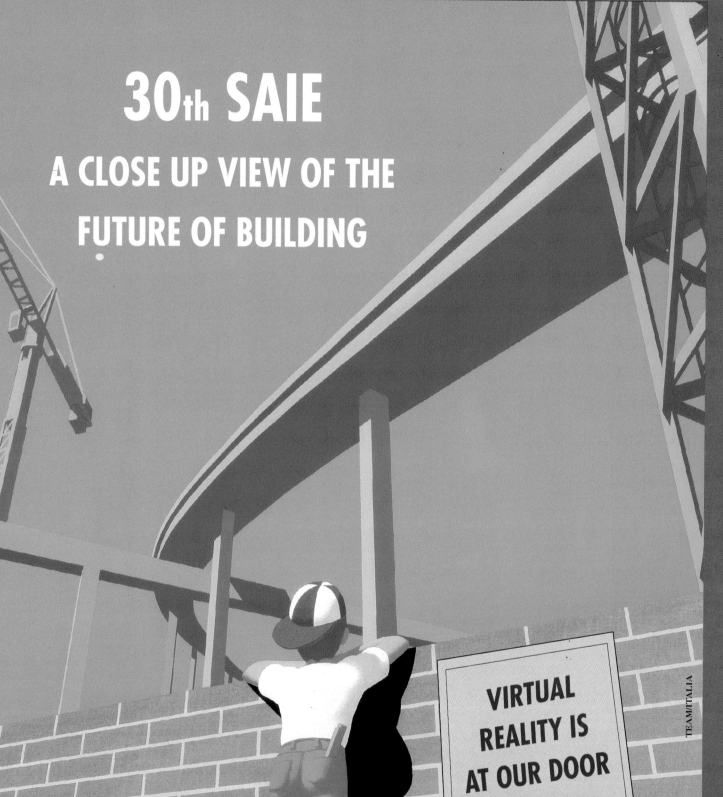

NEW TOWNS

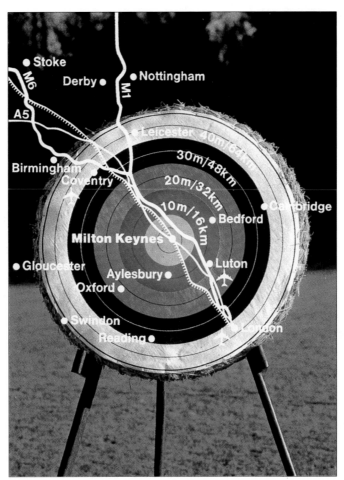

WHERE IS MILTON KEYNES?

Architectural Design

NEW TOWNS

ABOVE: NIGHT VIEW OF WILSHIRE CENTRE, LOS ANGELES; *OPPOSITE:* MILTON KEYNES, DRAWING BY PHILIP CASTLE

ACADEMY EDITIONS · LONDON

Acknowledgements

I would like to thank all contributors to this issue. Steen Eiler Rasmussen and Stephen Gardiner wrote their pieces some time ago – Stephen for the original *AD* on the city edited by Monica Pidgeon in 1973, Steen Eiler in 1990. Michael Brett's involvement over the years as a senior planner and associate with Llewelyn Davies and Derek Walker Associates puts him in a unique position as an observer of the development of Milton Keynes and a participant in major New Towns throughout the world. Martin Richardson's personal dedication to the development of public housing internationally is reflected in his critique of the Milton Keynes housing programme. Stuart Mosscrop's personal contribution to the city centre's elegant structure plan explains his distress at the excesses of the last decade. Finally David Lock, the British Government's Planning Adviser, gives a global view of international developments. Drawings included in the issue are by: Julian Baker, David Brimson, Neil Miller-Chalk, Helmut Jacoby, Aaron McCaffrey, Andrew Mahaddie, Stuart Mosscrop, David Reddick, John Seed, Wayland Tunley, Derek Walker, Peter Winchester, Christopher Woodward. John Donat acted as consultant photographer for the Development Corporation for the first eight years and many of the Milton Keynes illustrations are taken by him. Other photographers who have contributed to this *AD* are as follows: Michael Brett, John Csaky, Richard Davies, Ron Herron, Neil Higson, John Kelsey, Ken Kirkwood, Samantha Larrance, David Lock, Richard Murphy, John Nicolais, John Peck and Jo Reid, Derek Walker, Jan Walker, John Walker, John Willcocks.
Professor Derek Walker

Front Cover: 'The heart of Milton Keynes', Minale Tattersfield; *inside covers*: Walton Lake, Milton Keynes, drawing by Andrew Mahaddie

Photographic Credits
All material has been supplied courtesy of Derek Walker unless otherwise stated. Richard Bryant *p38 centre right*; City of Irvine *p89 above*; Peter Durant *p32 above left*, *p40 above and below left*; French Tourist Office pp85, 93 *centre right*; Dennis Gilbert *p32 above right*; Embassy of Finland *p90 below left and right*; Michel Denance *p95 below*

EDITOR: Maggie Toy
GUEST EDITOR: Derek Walker
EDITORIAL TEAM: Rachel Bean, Katherine MacInnes
ART EDITOR: Andrea Bettella CHIEF DESIGNER: Mario Bettella DESIGNER: Jan Richter

CONSULTANTS: Catherine Cooke, Terry Farrell, Kenneth Frampton, Charles Jencks
Heinrich Klotz, Leon Krier, Robert Maxwell, Demetri Porphyrios, Kenneth Powell, Colin Rowe, Derek Walker

First published in Great Britain in 1994 by *Architectural Design* an imprint of
ACADEMY GROUP LTD, 42 LEINSTER GARDENS, LONDON W2 3AN
Member of the VCH Publishing Group
ISBN: 1-85490-245-8 (UK)

Architectural Design Profile 111 is published as part of *Architectural Design* Vol 64 9-10/1994
Architectural Design Magazine is published six times a year and is available by subscription

Distributed to the trade in the United States of America by
ST MARTIN'S PRESS, 175 FIFTH AVENUE, NEW YORK, NY 10010

Printed and bound in Italy

Contents

RESORT DEVELOPMENT TELLURIDE, COLORADO, DEREK WALKER ASSOCIATES

ARCHITECTURAL DESIGN PROFILE No 111

NEW TOWNS

DEREK WALKER

INTRODUCTION

Following the publication of the Draft Master Plan for Milton Keynes in 1969, *Architectural Design* sensed that a singularly ambitious British initiative was in the offing.

For once Britain seemed to be making the right choices: the appointment of a dynamic and charismatic chairman, Lord Campbell of Eskan, who in turn assembled a board of wide ranging financial, social and political skills. Initially, for the critical local consultation period, Walter Ismay became the Corporation's first chief executive. He was exactly the right choice for that fraught and difficult process of endless consultation and reassurance that are so central to the British planning process. Campbell's appointment of Richard Llewellyn Davies was equally inspired. He, together with Walter Bor and John de Monchaux, produced a plan that was audacious, pragmatic and, in keeping with the sixties, not in the least doctrinaire. It proposed a low density solution with the dispersal of scarce resources and work places within a rough kilometre grid. However the speed of implementation proposed required specific skills and again Lord Campbell showed shrewd judgement. He recruited Fred Lloyd Roche, who already had a successful public service career in Coventry and Runcorn very much concerned with the sharp end of implementation. His appointment as successor to Walter Ismay in 1970 ensured that the Development Corporation had a formidable operator at the helm who understood the development process and was perhaps the best negotiator that the embryonic city could have had. He was an intensely ambitious and political animal whose staying power became legendary within the New Towns movement.

When I was rather surprisingly recruited from my Design orientated private practice, I was encouraged to bring design flair into the recruitment process. Strangely enough I had a very clear vision of the pattern I wanted to encourage. Perhaps naively I felt that control of the development process had to be design led, that our in-house team had to be run by designers, and that parallel to that we needed to establish a close working relationship with an external group of practices who could back up the efforts of the Development Corporation through direct commissions or shotgun marriages. What followed was an explosion of energy and idealistic commitment that was exciting and stimulating. The train was kept on the rails by the early appointment of Frank Henshaw as Chief Quantity Surveyor (he later succeeded Fred Roche as Chief Executive). His experience in setting up a realistic framework for development was vital, as were the local and national planning liaisons set up by Bill Berret, my deputy who commanded a fund of knowledge having worked on Pooley's alternative strategy for the designated area.

The design activity was intense. Local plans, village plans, citywide infrastructure and landscaping policies were developed. A system for industrial buildings and the structure of the city centre, conservation areas, housing programmes, community buildings, sport and recreation, health programmes, building classification and recruitment of a local building industry all ran parallel with national, local and county liaison.

The build up was to achieve one simple goal: 3,000 houses per year and enough support facilities to make the move for an incoming population to a new area less traumatic. Implementation of these policies demanded an exceptionally dynamic response and for that I am always grateful to all my colleagues. They were essentially a young team with all of us under 40, but energy coupled with experience dominated the key appointments. Tony Southard and Andrew Mahaddie led the group developing strategies for citywide landscape systems that form the backbone of the city structure, which were ably implemented in the late seventies and eighties by Neil Higson.

When I presented a concept for a city greener than the surrounding countryside to the board, 'Forest City' became our image, and after intense debate we allocated 20 per cent of the designated area to a citywide parkland system.

Barry Clayton and Derek Codling led the industry group searching for a system that elevated speculative factory buildings from the asbestos shed syndrome that prevailed at the time. Peter Winchester, John Seed and Dave Brimson led a village design group which produced the conservation document for the city and eleven village plans within a two year period. Nigel Lane and Wayland Tunley are inevitably associated with the development of northern Milton Keynes, sensitive infills in Stony Stratford and Wolverton to large housing schemes at

RIGHT: 'Forest City'

Fullers Slade, Neath Hill and Greenleys. Trevor Denton, Fred Higginson, Dave Byrne, Keith Revill and a very young David Reddick formed a group concentrating their efforts on the six grid squares adjacent to the centre housing 30,000 people. Jim Muldrew and Don Ritson led a team that included Ed Jones, Jeremy Dixon, Chris Cross, Mike Gold and Peter Barker who were concerned with major housing schemes in the south where tyrannical building systems and a lack of suitable building materials compromised both Netherfield and Coffee Hall.

The department's maverick quota was also kept fully occupied: Pierre Botschi wedded to GRP and Sherwood Drive, John Doggart to gaskets and energy conservation. Brian Milne developed children's play equipment and street furniture with Eric Maddox, Mike Glickman and Geoff Hollington. After early work with the landscape group John Czaky worked on elements of the Willen Lake project under Will Reuter and graduated to the highly successful Loughton Bowl Entertainment Area and its landscaped setting.

The City Centre Group led by Stuart Mosscrop and Chris Woodward and including Syd Green, Keith Barrell, Tony McKay and Brian Day created a superb area planning framework for development, whilst at the same time implementing the early offices, the shopping building and the basic infrastructure. This team was sustained by Monday evening design meetings, discussions and presentations, seminars by such luminaries as Buckminster Fuller and the irresistible conviction that everyone was working on a project that was unique and important.

The bubble of optimism was difficult to sustain. The first increase in oil prices sent shock waves through investors in 1973 and the three day week

in Heath's last term of office had similar effects. The success of the New Towns movement was based on comprehensive political support. Erosion of this principle started with Peter Shore's infamous Inner Cities versus New Towns debate. Michael Heseltine's doctrine of 'let the private sector build it' was doomed to failure both at the level of rolling programme and basic quality. Bankrupt and opportunist political doctrines are not sensible foundations for building anyone's future and the current decline in public values and concern for the public realm are coloured by underlying trends in a society that misguidedly believes that private interests and market forces will look after the environment.

Last year central government wound up Milton Keynes Development Corporation. It was successful commercially to the end and many of the early strategic planning and landscape design decisions have proved robust and sustainable. The filling in of the jigsaw puzzle has become less agreeable because of private sector pressure and a gradual wilting of the will to maintain strong development control. The most rewarding aspect of participation in the scheme was the sustained design education implicit in the whole process. Many of us have benefited so much from the privilege of helping create not an elitist cell but a habitat which, in Steen Eiler's words, is a vehicle for family development and growth.

As well as providing an epilogue to Milton Keynes this profile is concerned with parallel developments internationally that have drawn lessons from Milton Keynes and some which have not. Michael Brett and David Lock review these very different community approaches where density, climate and public ambition determine very different solutions.

STEEN EILER RASMUSSEN
REFLECTIONS ON MILTON KEYNES

Steen Eiler Rasmussen, in 1990, was updating his seminal work on 'London'. Milton Keynes was always in his eyes an orphan child of the capital's development and his continuing interest in the development from 1970 to his death last year was constant, supportive and perceptive. This piece, originally written in 1978 and updated in 1990, reflects his interest.

For me, a lifelong student of English planning, it has been a most intriguing experience to see Milton Keynes in the making, first to read the reports and study the whole philosophy behind the plans, and later to follow the progress in the field annually from 1972, and to have the privilege of discussing the implementation with members of the design team. This, the newest of all New Towns, is in many ways different from the general conception of an English New Town. It represents, in fact, a strong reaction to a number of the conventional principles, such as the centralised road system, the organisation in small neighbourhoods, the enclosing boundary; in short, all the sacred cows of the New Towns movement. But it is, nevertheless, a true child of that movement. It is only, as all sound children, critical of its descent. Thus, though Milton Keynes is a reaction to the New Towns theory as developed after World War II, it is still in keeping with the definition of the term 'Garden City' from before the War as adopted by the Council of the Garden Cities and Town Planning Association in 1920. That definition runs as follows: 'A Garden City is a town designed for healthy living and industry; of a size that makes possible a full measure of social life, but not larger; surrounded by a rural belt; the whole of the land being in public ownership or held in trust for the community.'

Milton Keynes is, in my opinion, an utterly English phenomenon, a link in a long chain of town planning experiments which started with the Garden City movement at the beginning of this century. It is an important contribution to a standing discussion and an answer to a number of questions which have been under debate for a long time. But it is also a continuation and perfection of the special London pattern of the 17th and 18th centuries that was so completely different from all continental city planning of the period.

The New Towns around London differ from Sir Ebenezer Howard's Garden City in one fundamental way. His self-contained town was conceived to have both industry and agriculture. Only one sixth of the whole area was reserved for the township, the rest was to remain as farmland surrounding the town, as an integral part of the complete Garden City. He wanted to create a balanced community with a balanced life where the farms supplied the whole area with food, thus minimising transport and transport costs, while the town sent back its waste products to the soil, thus increasing its fertility.

This great idea was, however, already Utopian in his lifetime and was never realised, not even in the first Garden Cities. English town planners have nevertheless stuck to the ideal of the comparatively small town surrounded on all sides by open land. It should satisfy the desire of townspeople for easy access to the beloved countryside. But if the town is also to be of a size that makes possible 'a full measure of social life', as Ebenezer Howard put it, it means, in modern times much larger towns, and it is then difficult to satisfy both wishes.

Howard, and many of his contemporaries, had a puritanical feeling that life in the small town must be healthier than in the larger one. I think we must see it otherwise. When so many people migrated to the cities, it was for very good reasons. They flocked to the place that could give them the best opportunities, and offer them the

ABOVE: Ideal City, Footfalls echo in the memory down the passage we did not take towards the door we never opened, Ben Johnson (acrylic on canvas); OPPOSITE: Strategic plan for Milton Keynes, Llewellyn Davies, Weeks, Forestier-Walker and Bor (1969)

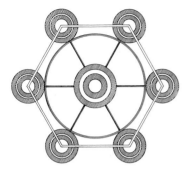

FROM ABOVE: Ebenezer
Howard's Correct Principle of a
City's Growth; maps showing
contours; parks

greatest variety of jobs, of commerce, of culture, learning and entertainment, and that was the large city and not the small self-contained town. How then can we satisfy both the demand for larger cities and the wish for easy access to the countryside?

Le Corbusier's answer was to concentrate the dwellings in some few skyscrapers standing like solitary trees in a large landscape and thus to 'recapture the horizon'. But what good – in the long run – can the horizon do to the man on the 20th floor?

By far the finest realisation of Le Corbusier's idea I have seen is the Roehampton Housing Estate, overlooking Richmond Deer Park. Here a number of detached high-rise buildings, standing amongst centuries old trees in a large green valley, form a beautiful landscape. It is indeed fine to look at, and it makes good photographs. But is it satisfactory for the ordinary English family to live in? Is it enough to be idle figures in a fine picture? In Harlow New Town it has been easier to rent out cottages than flats, even where the latter have been attractively situated. Thus Le Corbusier's vision of modern town life seems not to be the right one for the English.

Another solution is the linear town with its limitless growth and short distance to the countryside from any point of the plan. This will, on the other hand, mean long distances inside the city itself.

The following question then arises: are the English, after all, so interested in close contact with the countryside that they will sacrifice other conveniences for it? I think not. What they really want is not so much the *look* of fine landscapes as ample possibilities for an open air life in attractive surroundings.

This has led to that specific English device, the London landscape/parkland inside the town; not town-parks like those you can find in Germany or France with 'Keep off the Grass' signs, but old hunting grounds such as St James's Park, Hyde Park, Regent's Park or Hampstead Heath, preserved for the public, places where you can feel as free as in a piece of untouched nature, although you are really in a carefully maintained public park. It is better to live on the border of Regent's Park with all its facilities for games and sports, than in the middle of the Roehampton Park.

From these premises it seems the right conclusion that Milton Keynes was planned first of all for a larger population than the other New Towns, and secondly that the inner parkland like a preserved piece of nature is supplemented with a number of local sportsfields and playgrounds evenly distributed over the residential areas.

The consultant planners have learned the lesson from the New Towns not to start with too detailed a planning that might become obsolete before it is realised. What a new town needs right from the start is more a clear strategy for the procedure than a proper planning. It needs a great framework, inside which there can be freedom for the future development of local areas.

This framework has the form of a network of primary roads for today's most common means of transport, the private motor car, which is both a great convenience and a great nuisance. It can quickly transport people from door to door, thus minimising the distances of a widespread city. But all these cabins on wheels use too much power and take up too much space for just bringing single persons from one part of the city to another, and the private car is furthermore dangerous, noisy and air polluting. It is therefore of vital interest for the future city to have an overall network which might utilise the best qualities of the car and reduce its defects. It can then be hoped that such a road plan may also be suitable for the better means of transport which the future may bring. (There is already one in action – the 'dial-a-bus' system, which functions well in the road system.)

A centralised plan as originally proposed by Sir Ebenezer Howard and carried out in all London New Towns must inevitably lead to congested traffic at the centre, where there is least space for it. The Milton Keynes great road system has therefore avoided any specific road centre and has the form of a square grid. After careful studies and traffic calculations, it has been decided to use one kilometre squares, thus dividing the land into a number of smaller units, each of which has only local traffic. This results in a segregation of traffic, a hierarchy of roads from fast through-roads down to the small local lanes, bicycle tracks and walks. Pedestrians and bicycles have no access to the great grid roads and can cross them only by underpasses or bridges. The grid roads are thus reserved for the motor car, which, however, can slow down to the speed of the local traffic and show consideration for the quiet life in a residential area.

The traffic on the grid roads can, in the future, be regulated by a system of traffic lights at crossings so arranged that a car can pass along the same road without stopping when it has come into what the Americans call 'a green wave'.

This grid system should thus avoid congestion at focal points (as there *are* no focal points), facilitate fast driving on long distances, and reduce the danger of accidents where different kinds of traffic meet.

The system has also considered the other evils of motor traffic, namely those of noise and air pollution. The grid roads are planned to be bordered with trees, not municipal standard trees as used on boulevards and avenues, but a real thicket of trees, different trees, some taller than any building in the town with smaller trees and bushes under and between them, filling out all openings, together forming gigantic hedges, green walls on both sides of the road. They screen off the noise of the traffic, being most effective where they are planted on earth banks or ramparts. Still the noise from a motor road with no obstacles will not be serious. A much greater fear is the air pollution and that is where the trees have their important mission. A Norwegian research report has published the following results. A full-grown tree with a crown-diameter of about 14 metres has a total leaf-surface of 1,600 square metres. It uses the coal-dioxides in the air, breaks down sulphur dioxides and produces in one growth period enough oxygen to satisfy the need of one man for a year. The same tree filters up to one tonne of dust a year, thus binding soot and bacteria etc. It is therefore a most rational solution to let the fast cars pass through tunnels of trees which can absorb the noxious gases produced by the motors.

The system of dividing up the urban area into units of square kilometres is not intended to be a pattern of orthodox 'neighbourhoods'. On the contrary, the grid combined with the local road systems should give the inhabitants freedom to move over the entire city, thus taking advantage of 'the full measure of social life' which the city can offer them.

Each person is at liberty to live in his individual unplanned neighbourhood. For the baby it is the family, the house and garden; the infant captures the whole local road and the playground with his playmates; the schoolchild has a still larger domain; and finally the adults' neighbourhood is wholly determined by their way of living, their work and friends. I feel sure that the flexibility and freedom of the Milton Keynes plan will suit most people better than those pre-planned neighbourhoods that try to impose a provincial way of life on all, whether they like it or not.

Coming to Milton Keynes in 1977, it was extremely difficult to perceive any comprehensive image of the whole area and even more of the city which would eventually cover it. Milton Keynes was then like an enormous patchwork with only some of the patches placed. But the landscape has some great features which the urban developments should enhance and not conceal.

A contour map shows the land as an undulating landscape with a ridge coming from the southeast and going north in the middle of the designated area, with a valley on both sides. At the bottom of the west valley is the small Loughton Brook running north to the River Ouze, while the eastern valley is drained by the Grand Union

Canal and the River Ouzel, which is also a tributary of the Ouze. These two valleys will, with their undulating waters, traverse the man-made grid and form a delightful contrast to it.

These valleys, which are no good as building sites, will naturally be the inner parkland, where man, tired of townlife, can have a carefree walk following the natural paths, revealing a new view at every bend and leading to all sorts of lovely recreation, a golf course, playing fields, old village greens and lakes.

The two linear parks are connected to the city centre, riding over the ridge from one side to the other. The commercial centre is a most ambitious scheme; a huge, regular rectangular building surrounded by rectangular, urban avenues of plane trees and parking spaces. Seen from an aesthetic point of view, I find it a happy solution to crown the height – and thereby the whole city – with such a large, regular structure, a module of the grid system. Its axis leads to the city park, a hilly, green landscape overlooking the valley, the lakes and the distant countryside. This is, for me, the real English Landscape Park, the legacy of William Kent, Chambers and the others who, in the seventeenth and eighteenth centuries, opened up secluded gardens into great vistas.

The whole city centre with its great structures had to be very regular and the grid up there was consequently changed from a less formal road system to a more rigid one of straight lines and right angles. Curved roads, in these circumstances, would have been simply ridiculous and would have meant a great waste of the most valuable land in Milton Keynes.

The regularity of the city centre is again reflected in the neighbouring housing development called Fishermead. It looks very convincing here with its square, its central street with the great city centre building as a *point de vue* and its rectangular housing courts.

This normative form of the most important part of the whole of Milton Keynes must, in my opinion, inevitably lead to a discussion of the form of the overall grid.

When I got to know the concept of Milton Keynes from the preliminary report of 1968, and its presentation by Lord Richard Llewellyn Davies in *Town Planning Review*, and in the *Architectural Review* article in August 1969, I felt that it was a great step forward from the New Towns with their artificial naturalness. It was a relief to see a civilised plan again.

We have to use our imagination to foresee what Milton Keynes will be like in our grandchildren's

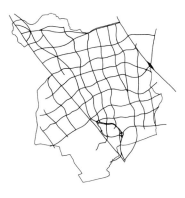

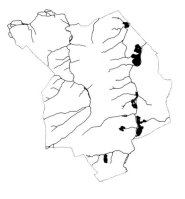

FROM ABOVE: Ed Ruscha, City, lithograph; maps showing grid road and water courses; LEFT: Grid road planting policy

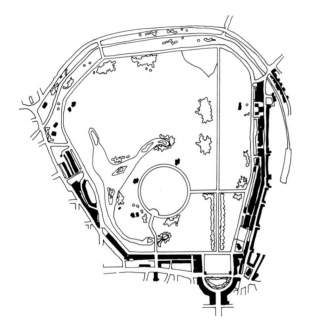

time. Some roads will be like forest roads, but where there are landmarks or where the road passes parkland, there will be openings in the tall 'hedges' bordering the road.

There is at Aspley Heath (between Woburn and Woburn Sands), a road through a thick wood. The road is slightly curved – not more than those grid roads that have already been executed – and you cannot see very far ahead as you drive along. I find it very pleasant there, but I would not like a city with many roads like that. Where you cannot see anything at the sides, it is important to have a deep vista in front of you, otherwise you will feel locked up in a maze, lose your orientation and suffer from claustrophobia.

When I saw the planned proposals and early implementation by Derek Walker and his design team it reinforced my confidence in their work. They had gone some way to making sure that the city would have an infrastructure and landscape quality totally unique in the New Town's history.

This talented group of dedicated young designers had perceived that in an imperfect and democratic world where development agencies do not and cannot control absolute quality of either individual projects or building groups that they should hopefully seek to control the spaces between buildings and the basic infrastructure. Walker's personal commitment to a green city manifests itself most significantly in the city centre where three heavily planted and spacious boulevards are linked to a linear parks system which with the grid road reservations will provide the city with its character.

This network of green, occupying almost 20 per cent of the city's acreage reminds me of one of my great loves: The Royal Parks of London. At Milton Keynes these green lungs integrate the old settlements into the new city fabric with sensitivity and style.

The 'open plan' of Milton Keynes is, in my opinion, not so shockingly new as many people think. Its pattern reminds me most of all of the West End of London in the seventeenth and eighteenth centuries, with its kilometre grid of through-roads – Piccadilly, Oxford Street and later Marylebone Road, Bond Street and Park Lane; and its great housing estates built between the roads – Covent Garden, the first Bloomsbury and other London squares with access to the special English landscape park such as St James's, Hyde Park and Regent's Park.

If the building up of Milton Keynes is not disturbed too much by pre-conceived ideas of what a city should be like, but implemented with consistency, it should be a city that could satisfy all the needs of the town dwellers and have a greater variety of things to offer than most cities in the world. From the city centre, the great mart, which is the core of city life, you can go down to the residential squares. Each is a neat little local town with all its little houses and gardens, but with a protecting backdrop of great trees, full of bird life. You can come to working places, to the Open University, to all sorts of social activities. You can also drop into real provincial towns like Stony Stratford, or into the old villages which, with their churches, pubs and greens, adapt themselves to the city as has, for instance, Bethnal Green to London. And you can feel at ease in the linear parks.

The present Milton Keynes seems to attract people of all social strata, skilled as well as unskilled labourers, academic people and non-academics. It is a good omen for its growth and development. Because the city is, after all, not the roads, trees and houses, but the people.

LEFT: Man-made lake at Willen, linear park; OPPOSITE FROM ABOVE L TO R: Plan of Stowe; Holland Park, London; plan of Regent's Park, London; Regent's Park; plan of St James's Park, London; St James's Park

MICHAEL BRETT
IN THE FROZEN NORTH

The first *Architectural Design* special edition on Milton Keynes came out in the summer of 1973 when I was a few years into my first job as a young architect-planner in the Euston Road. For my friends and me that issue was something you had to have, rather like the latest album from Pink Floyd, which in some respects it resembled. Many of the more interesting of my fellow AA graduates of the late 1960s had gathered at Wavendon Tower under Derek Walker, and there they all were on the front cover, dishevelled, anorexic-looking to a large extent, many for some reason wearing black and perching like crows in the branches of an ancient elm-tree. We had already seen something of what was going on in a beguiling exhibition at the Design Centre in 1972, designed to give the Development Corporation six weeks of national exposure in their search for investors and employers. There was a sewage works of exceptional elegance complete with giant Archimedes screw, and modelled in silver. A complete and innovative system for industrial buildings had been designed. Some very serious thought was going into large-scale landscape structures evoking the eighteenth-century work of Repton and Brown. Familiar items such as schools, play areas, and sports centres had been completely rethought both in organisation and design. With the co-operation of the residents, complete plans had been developed for all the existing villages. The list of consultants circling round the Wavendon team was deeply impressive – Colquhoun and Miller, Evans and Shalev, Erskine, Rogers, Foster and Stirling. The architecture was cool, airy and disciplined. Given the generation it would take to build the new city, we all felt that here in what Buckinghamshire Councillors used to call the 'Frozen North', the most talented of our designers, working within the discipline of the cleverest plan for a major new development since the war, would be given the time and resources to come up with a sparkling demonstration of what we could do in the mid-twentieth century in British urban planning and design.

The Greek philosopher and physiologist Alcmaeon wrote 'men perish because they cannot connect the beginning with the end'. Nowhere is this more true than in the case of the great British public project, and in undertaking the design and construction of a new city any society embarks on a revolutionary, exacting and mysterious process. As a human artifact the city defies description unless you are a poet or a painter. Certainly the attempts of 'urbanism' to discover in city life, as in nature, systems of cause and effect which can be used to change the outcome of the story have not always had encouraging results. Nor should this surprise us, for the briefest excursion into the urban 'sciences' must give us pause to wonder how far we dare to proceed. First we have the ageless 'Utopian' ideal which, as Meyerson has pointed out, has rarely succeeded in reconciling the idea of the perfect society with the image of the ideal city as a physical entity. Then we have the operation of the 'market' – in land, floorspace, goods, ideas and information – a mechanism of infinite complexity, perhaps the basis of all urban life, but nowhere well understood. Finally we have not only the behavioural sciences which attempt to explain how city life works in social terms but also numerous technologies – of transport, building, communications and so on.

Even as we attempt to arrange all this in some sort of comprehensive framework of knowledge, ideas and principles, over time we are confronted, especially in a democracy, with the gradual erosion of whatever consensus there was on goals and priorities, and hence of the will needed to see the project through to completion. All this makes the survival of Milton Keynes through nearly 30 years of political, social and economic upheaval in itself something of a miracle and since nothing comparable is likely to be attempted again in the UK we are presented in the Frozen North with a rare opportunity to explore the utility of the long term planning process itself; whether the kind of forecasts, intentions and concepts that have to be assembled at the outset can remain relevant for a generation and whether it is possible to follow through a sustained and consistent programme of development in which the original ideas remain in focus.

It is curious that successive governments have so doggedly persisted with the project. The great policy debates of the golden age of regional planning, *c*1960-75, which continued the postwar efforts to manage growth in the London region, are long forgotten. Who now remembers the new cities proposed for Newbury and Southampton, the two other elements in the triumvirate

LEFT: Milton Keynes team (1973)

FROM ABOVE L TO R: Designated Area from Bow Brickhill (1970); children's play equipment (1971); Calverton End housing, internal courtyard; aerial view of Linford Manor group; Poplar Walk; pavement/cycleway at Linford

of 'third wave' London New Towns, neither of which ever saw the light of day? 'Overspill', nowadays, is something that happens after your third pint at the Barge and Whistle. Into the dustbin with regional planning, public housing and the New Towns programme has gone practically every other effort we have made to think big and to think long term, including all attempts to look strategically at our airports, transport and housing.

Yet Milton Keynes has survived not only the demise of the policy framework that gave birth to it, but also repeated efforts by powerful enemies to kill it off. In 1970, before anything much had happened on site, the threat of a gigantic four-runway airport loomed from Cublington in the Vale of Aylesbury to the south. In the mid 1970s, against a background of economic collapse and housing cuts, Peter Shore diverted much of what funds were available to the inner cities, accusing Milton Keynes of enticing workers and employers away from London, one of the purposes for which it had been created. During the next decade, successive Conservative Secretaries of State, beginning with Michael Heseltine who signed the death warrant of the Development Corporation in 1981, engineered a complete reversal of the ethos of the new city. Out went public housing for rent, 'social balance' and the traditional dependence on grant-in-aid. In came 'cash limits' and a fire sale of the cities assets, still in progress when the Development Corporation was wound up in 1992. The survival of Milton Keynes over the decades despite media ridicule, government subversion, and several personality changes owes a great deal to the political skills and single-mindedness of Jock Campbell, Chairman of the Development Corporation until he retired in 1983 just as the age of Thatcherism, in which he felt deeply uncomfortable, was gathering momentum.

Much is owed also to the durability of the master plan for the new city. By the time the team of consultants under Richard Llewellyn Davies, Walter Bor and John de Monchaux was officially appointed in 1967, Campbell and Llewellyn Davies were already engaged in a wide ranging debate on the key assumptions that would ultimately produce a structure for the new city. The intellectual underpinnings of the familiar and seminal grid layout were established during an intensive three month 'goals formulation' process, kicked off at a dinner at the Hyde Park Hotel in the first week of December 1967. Not only was this process in itself an innovation, in that for the first time in British planning it set out to paint a picture of the kind of society for which the new city would be built, 20 or 30 years hence, but it led to ideas for the new city which were revolutionary, reflecting in particular the restless intellect of Richard Llewellyn Davies, his awareness of current research and writing outside the cosy English

urban and academic circles, and his impatience with all previous efforts at New Town planning in the UK which he regarded as unsophisticated and lacking any real theoretical basis.

For the completely new start and the more penetrating understanding of the way cities really work, which he felt were needed, Llewellyn Davies had drawn on the heterogeneous network of sources he had cultivated in British and American universities as Professor at the Bartlett School, many of them outside the planning and architecture disciplines. These included Jane Jacobs whose recently published books on planning failures in Baltimore and New York were becoming known to British planners, the writings of the British social scientist Terence Lee, and the work of Christopher Alexander, a Berkeley mathematician who had analysed conventional New Town plans using a notation from the Theory of Sets – something which many British architects had heard of by late 1967, if few could understand it. Alexander's diagrams showed what he called a 'tree', with a hierarchy of linkages from leaf to branch to trunk to root, whereas the reality of urban life was represented for him by infinitely complex sets of linkages which he tried to represent mathematically and called a 'lattice'. Melvin Webber, Professor of Urban and Regional Planning at Berkeley, who participated in the goals formulation process, had been arguing since 1964 that the network of interactions within the city was much more complex than planners had hitherto thought, probably more complex than was capable of analysis: that the purpose of urbanisation was to provide access to information and opportunity, and the purpose of planning was to maximise the diversity of information and range of opportunities available to the citizen.

The Llewellyn Davies team was impressed by this growing body of evidence that the planner's traditional classification of land uses and identification of 'neighbourhoods' and other ephemera such as the building blocks of towns and cities was at odds with the richness, complexity and variety of city life, and this made previous efforts at New Town planning in Britain seem a crude and unsympathetic process driven by faulty analysis and image-making. They saw the city as seamless, a 'field of possibilities', in principle without boundary, hierarchy or focus, its major functions undifferentiated as far as possible, evenly distributed across a neutral framework of routes giving equivalent standards of access in all areas, adaptable, and flexible in the speed and direction of expansion.

What resulted in practical terms was the familiar one kilometre grid of medium sized roads laid like a fishnet across the rather sombre north Buckinghamshire landscape; consistent low to medium residential densities and, to even out traffic flow, concentrations of employment in the

ABOVE: Olivetti Concourse, James Stirling and Partner (1971)

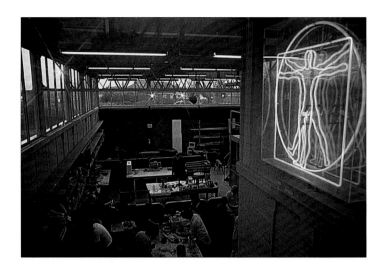
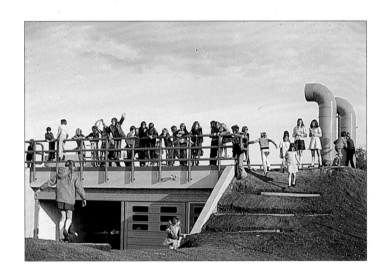

FROM ABOVE L TO R: Melrose Avenue Activity Centre, Colquhoun
and Miller (1971); Galley Hill, workshop, MKDC (1972); Calverton
Children's play area, Archigram (1973); Wolverton Sports Club,
MKDC (1972); Bletchley street market, MKDC (1973); Dial-a-Bus – a
convenient bus/taxis service for pioneers (1971)

main commercial centre and scattered industrial areas. Use of private cars was not to be constrained, as it had been in earlier New Towns, by congestion and lack of parking. There would, however, be a public transport system based on small buses running on grid roads which would offer a competitive service for those without the means, inclination or ability to drive.

The Llewellyn Davies team knew that these proposals could prove vulnerable to the erosion of government will and consistency over time, as well as to the normal cycle of elation and despair in the broader economy and the difficulties inherent in long term forecasting in an era of continuous and rapid change. It was for this reason that 'robustness' and 'adaptability' were seen as crucial to the plan's long term viability; but it was also made clear to the planners that there was an important policy context to their work, and that clear social and economic goals would have to be met.

It was the adaptability of the idea in the light of the array of outside pressures, many of them both unwelcome and unexpected, which would come to bear on the growth and development of the city, which partly accounts for its survival. The question is whether this adaptability has simply made it easier for succeeding governments to divert the project from the course on which it was originally set. In a way the plan for Milton Keynes, though conceived in a public sector corporatist environment, brilliantly anticipated the rise of the freewheeling market-driven economy of the 1980s, a decade in which professional planners increasingly found themselves asked to re-direct their focus from the regulation of urban growth to the stimulation of development by any and every means available. Many of the more high-minded principles of the 1960s were cast adrift. The goal of a 50 per cent public sector:50 per cent private sector housing ratio was killed off by the destruction of the 'social' housing programme in 1980. In the 1990s it is questionable whether anyone knows, or cares, what effect this has had on the 'social structure' of the new city; but in the late winter of 1968 this subject gave rise to a succession of carefully crafted technical papers from the planning team one of whose worries, ironically, was how middle class workers could be encouraged to move to the new city, as they had not been to earlier New Towns.

We can explore the problem further by looking at the way transport has evolved in Milton Keynes. It is not that car ownership has failed to reach the levels forecast in 1967; the current national figure of 0.37 cars per person is impressively close to the figure of 0.35 forecast by the master plan transport consultants. The difficulty is that the substantial subsidies which would inevitably have been needed at Milton Keynes to develop a public transport system to a point where it could offer a competitive service have never been forthcoming. As a consequence, by necessity rather than choice (contrary to the intentions of the planning team), car ownership in Milton Keynes, at 80 per cent of households, is considerably higher than the national figure of 67 per cent. Use of the bus system for work trips at about 5 per cent has to be compared with the 30 per cent which the planners felt could be reached if public transport were to offer an attractive option to travellers. The city has more than its share of obsolete, poorly maintained cars belching pollutants into the atmosphere and it has become possible to portray the 'city of the future' as environmentally 'unsustainable' and a major consumer of resources, particularly land and energy.

So we live in a world very different from the one into which Milton Keynes was born. Nor should this surprise us. As Plato wrote, 'nothing ever is, all is becoming'. Over time, all cities must adjust to the purposes each generation finds for them and this is no less true of New Towns and cities simply because in the first instance they are designed to achieve socially useful goals largely at public expense. For better or worse, Milton Keynes has at least partially fulfilled its mandate of absorbing development pressures which might otherwise have added to the problems of more vulnerable parts of the region; and it would be faint-hearted to suggest that we should not attempt to deal with problems and opportunities in urban development which it will take a generation to resolve.

So, given the fuzziness and uncertainty of their horizons, the planning consultants cannot be faulted for having presented to the implementation team at Wavendon a flexible framework which gave them considerable latitude in the ways in which they turned a diagram into a city. The question is whether they could, or should, have been even less prescriptive than they were. It is surely a valid criticism of the plan that, from the perspective of the 1990s, it cannot apparently be adapted to sustain a valid and competitive public transport system, other than at unacceptable public cost. A plan that was less prescriptive particularly in its later phases might have made it easier to focus employment and higher residential densities in ways reflecting both the declining household sizes and market trends toward rented accommodation which we are likely to see in the next decades, and a desire to organise development in ways better suited to a sustainable public transport system.

In mid May Milton Keynes is a lovely place. There is no other word for it. The implementation team have unquestionably succeeded in their aim of finding a visual language for uniformly low densities. The 'city in a forest' of the 1973 diagrams is fast becoming a reality. Already by 1984 there were several hundred established

FROM ABOVE: Watling Way School, Bucks County Council (1972); model for Milton Keynes village housing, MKDC (1972)

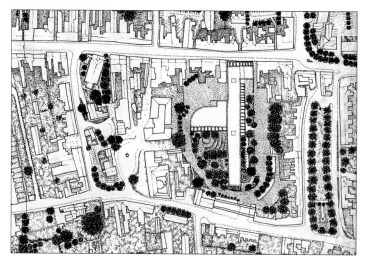

community organisations in the new city including no fewer than 65 soccer clubs, seven tennis clubs, 11 squash clubs, associations for five types of Martial Arts, the Woughton Park Ladies Badminton Club, the 'Wild Bunch' Western Society, the Milton Keynes Scottish Country Dance Association and the Concrete Cow Folk Club. On an evening walk through the Ouzel Valley park this week I passed a balloon landing, a cricket match (complete with unsuccessful appeal for LBW) and two nesting families of swans. Currently at the general hospital the grandchildren of the early pioneers are being born. Even if we do not altogether know what the word means we know that the city has become a community. This alone is something of an achievement.

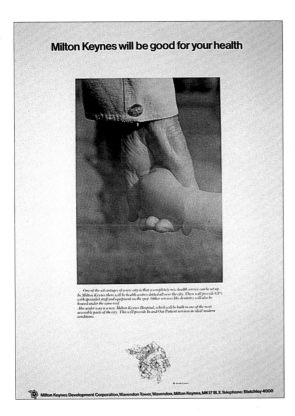

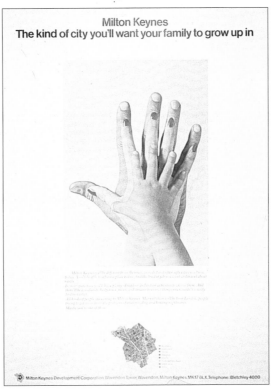

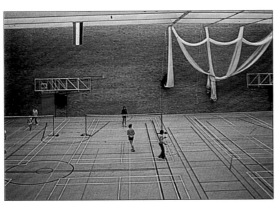

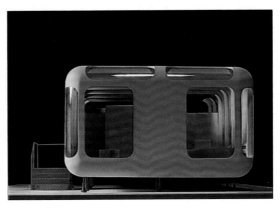

FROM ABOVE L TO R: Model of linear parks; posters for Milton Keynes, Minale Tattersfield (1972-75); Bletchley Leisure Centre, Faulkner Brown (1971); GRP housing for construction industry, MKDC (1972); OPPOSITE FROM ABOVE L TO R: Woolstones River Bank; Cofferidge Close housing and offices, MKDC; Cofferidge Close, plan, MKDC; Central Area Housing, Plateau Court, MKDC; Springfield Local Centre, MKDC; Great Linford Village, MKDC

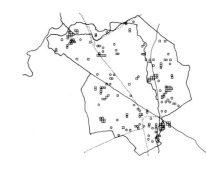

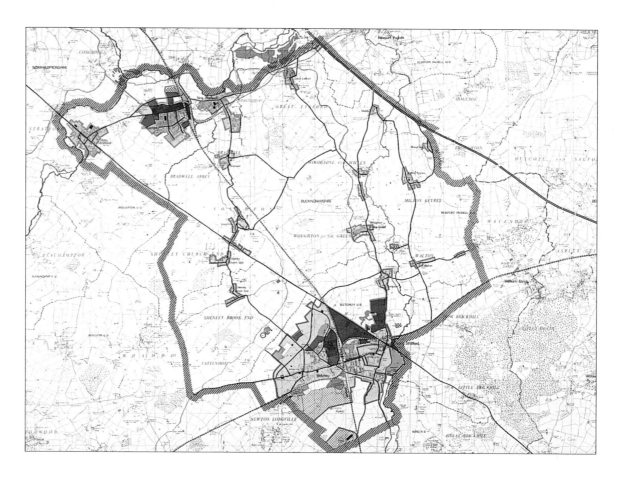

STEPHEN GARDINER
THE CITY AS A RUG

Stephen Gardiner's article was published in the June 1973 edition of Architectural Design. *It anticipated the scope of the landscape intentions and still provides insights into the use of landscape as a structuring device so central to the implementation of Milton Keynes.*

W H Auden once wrote: 'The earth turns over, our side feels cold . . .' It struck me suddenly that this marvellous image describes the huge stretch of land round Milton Keynes where the Development Corporation is going to build the new city. The first impression of north Buckinghamshire is of open, empty country where there seems to be no shelter, where all signs of life in lighted windows and cottage smoke appear to have been blown away by a big wind – a bare, chill landscape: you want to pull a rug over it to keep it warm. And this picture suggests, perhaps, the most profound interest of this extraordinary project: an addition is being made to a place that requires an addition. The city will be the rug.

But when you look closer you start coming across the scatterings of detail over the shoulders of hills – bits of the English past. The muddle of old village high streets, Norman towers, manor houses, eccentricities in ironwork, the Grand Union canal, bridges, streams, clumps of trees and meandering footpaths. In parts, there is, after all, quite an intricate mosaic – some lovely architecture, some really massive ancient hedges – from which to continue and to which to add, to enrich; but not to spoil, nor to subtract from the scene. This is the material; not unlike an eighteenth-century map of some place now covered over – St John's Wood or Regent's Park in London – as it was before the great estates filled the gaps, the market gardens and the fields, and ran terraces behind the avenues along the lanes. This is the delicate and sensitive picture which the architects, planners and engineers enter at Milton Keynes.

You stand back, take another look from a long way off: the diagrammatic and distant view of a city here shows a sequence of overlays that do not disrupt the landscape's origins, its indigenous and natural life. One overlay, for instance, describes a pattern of roads – not quite a grid, more a fish net which traps the city area in its mesh – and these roads, in turn, describe the positions of different neighbourhoods, the centre with its markets and offices and entertainment, the park and villages. The next overlay reveals some of the detail: the complex variations in the arrangement of residential neighbourhoods surrounding the city centre, and in the arrangements of settlements in the vicinity of villages, the shape and size of the lakes in the park, a line of poplars marking out a curve in the canal, a curved terrace pegging the position of another, the uninterrupted paths of trees and old hedges wandering through the new straight streets, hedges and gardens of Coffeehall. Then comes the overlay which brings the design of the structures at the centre, and the surrounding neighbourhood, into sharp architectural focus – a glass roof vaults an ice-rink, an orangery and a swimming pool with a single movement, avenues of trees invade the arcades leading to the shops mixed in with flats and offices, dense boulevards enclose the whole. This overlay begins to make real images in the mind, and at this point you make a discovery: when all the overlays are placed above each other it is the green of Nature which transcends all else through the layers of tracing paper. Nature is the frame for Milton Keynes, just as it was, once upon a time, the frame for New Haven in Connecticut and is still in parts of Paris. One day, when the trees have grown really big and round it will be upon Nature that this city will finally depend for its humanity and order.

And so Nature provides the structure from which to continue, and from which the architecture will grow, and this structure is, of course, an extension of what is already there. But it provides an umbrella of trees as well, and it is beneath these that everything happens – the houses, the shops, the boating on the canal, the schools, the paths and gardens. The additions to Nature are, however, carefully calculated, and by increasing the intensity of the landscape, by creating more things to do and more places to go, a much greater variety will be dug out of the ground. The variations in Nature can be endless, and the architects, inspired by this thought, carry on where Nature leaves off. The residential neighbourhoods round the centre are a particularly outstanding example of the struggle to discover variety, although not in such a way that the unity of the whole shall be disrupted.

To maintain this unity, the variations have their roots in a simple and unmistakable classical theme. Each neighbourhood is based on a square form and this is occupied by 500-600 people – numbers vary so that it can correspond to the architectural scheme, which in itself varies considerably within the discipline and outline of the square. For instance, there is the square that is entirely composed of one-storey houses with walled courtyard gardens, and the houses themselves vary considerably – some are for single people, some for married, some for families of different sizes. The effect of this group will be flat with trees and bushes poking up out of the courtyards, and the walls of the lanes which divide the interior of the square into parts will be covered with creepers like ivy. And so here, in essence, is the Greek village plan of, say, 200 BC. Next to it there may be the more familiar square that one associates with the eighteenth-century tradition. This form is secured with terraces, or with detached houses, or, in some squares, semidetached, or a mixture. Unlike the Georgian square, however, the main road that connects the houses is on the outside, and this reverses the house and garden plan, and establishes a safe 'green' in the middle for children. Yet the internal road of the Georgian square still remains – to allow vans in, thus attracting movement and other variations to the interior, again recalling the Georgian plan where the square was often closed from the main road with gates.

Then there is another example of the classical tradition: the terraces, the courtyard mosaic, the semi-detached houses suddenly contract, rearranging themselves as an apartment block in the centre of the square surrounded by flat grass and trees – Le Corbusier's Villa Savoie lying in its field outside Poissy, the cube in its space. This cube closely follows Corbusier's discoveries within the form – the interior is dug out leaving a courtyard behind at the centre and a skeleton of balconies and double-storeys on the facade: again, there are variations, but the outline of the cube remains, actively controlling this addition to the landscape, this object among trees – from the wings. In principle, it differs little from the garden surrounded by terraces or houses; for there the architectural composition, focusing on the garden, is glued together by the sides. At the apartment block it is the focus on the cube in its green square which is the architectural composition; this was Le Corbusier's point.

Here are some of the ideas that are being worked out at Milton Keynes. Many others are just as remarkable – combinations of terraces and crescents, of one-storey patterns and bigger things. The work goes on, relentlessly; the search for total integration, for an ordered whole. How has it been done? What is the 'force that drives the green fuse'? The truth is, I believe, very simple. Milton Keynes (its conception, its design) mirrors the minds that are creating it, and a method of working. If this city is, as an idea, an integrated whole it is because the minds that are making it have combined to create an integrated whole. Somewhere, for once, Nature seems to be operating the pulleys in the background, and this shows in the transcendency of Nature at the end of the day – boulevards connect the city with the country, and streets with houses, and people with people. It is Nature which 'drives the green fuse'.

Llewellyn Davies and his partners made a very good overall plan, and it was good because it was reticent enough to accept changes and variations without damage to its fundamental order. Then there is the Board under Lord Campbell, who with General Manager Fred Lloyd Roche, support and encourage all being done by Derek Walker and his design department. And there is more to this than there sounds: for this Board is supporting and encouraging an approach to the profound depths of city planning which is as unique as it is unconventional in England today.

LEFT: Major landscaping policies were important from the outset. A three-dimensional green matrix was formed by earth mounding and tree masses. These ingredients, predominantly related to traffic routes, existing woodlands and major topographical features, combine with an overlay proposing a linear park, footpath and cycleway system to complement the grid road landscaping channels. Major landscaping was to provide coherence, linkage and the prime indicator of the eventual city 'ideal'.

The plan envisaged reservations and planting for which there were no precedents in existing New Towns. The character of a dispersed, low density city is the cumulative product of a number of elusive factors, such as a general impression of woodland, greenery and a relaxed generosity of scale. Built piecemeal over a number of years, the infrastructure elements – services, roads, landscape – were the only elements over which the Corporation had long-standing control, thus control of landscape provided important visual continuity. The landscape design policy was generated not by buildings, grid scale or land use, but by major topographical features and sector scale planning. The necessity of protective continuous planting and mounding on the grid roads works together with visual intelligibility on a larger scale. The planting policy concentrated on plants native to lowland Britain, created large species zones to give a sense of location with local variety and attention to future planting requirements. One forest tree species, one small tree and one shrub have been allocated to each zone, to form the dominant species (at least 70 per cent of the mix). FROM ABOVE L TO R: Landscape policy precedents: Letchworth; Broadacre City; La Ville Radieuse; Milton Keynes; overlays showing movement and physical form: roads; topography; sectors; sub grid; grid; super grid; planting zones – (1) Stantonbury: lime, birch, hawthorn (2) northern towns and Shenleys: ash, hazel, snowberry (3) city centre: horse chestnut, yew, laurel (4) Woughton and Bletchley: Norway maple, field maple, blackthorn (5) Milton Keynes and Willen: turkey oak, wild cherry, myrobalan plum (6) river valleys and linear parks: white and goat willow, dogwood; protective planting along roads

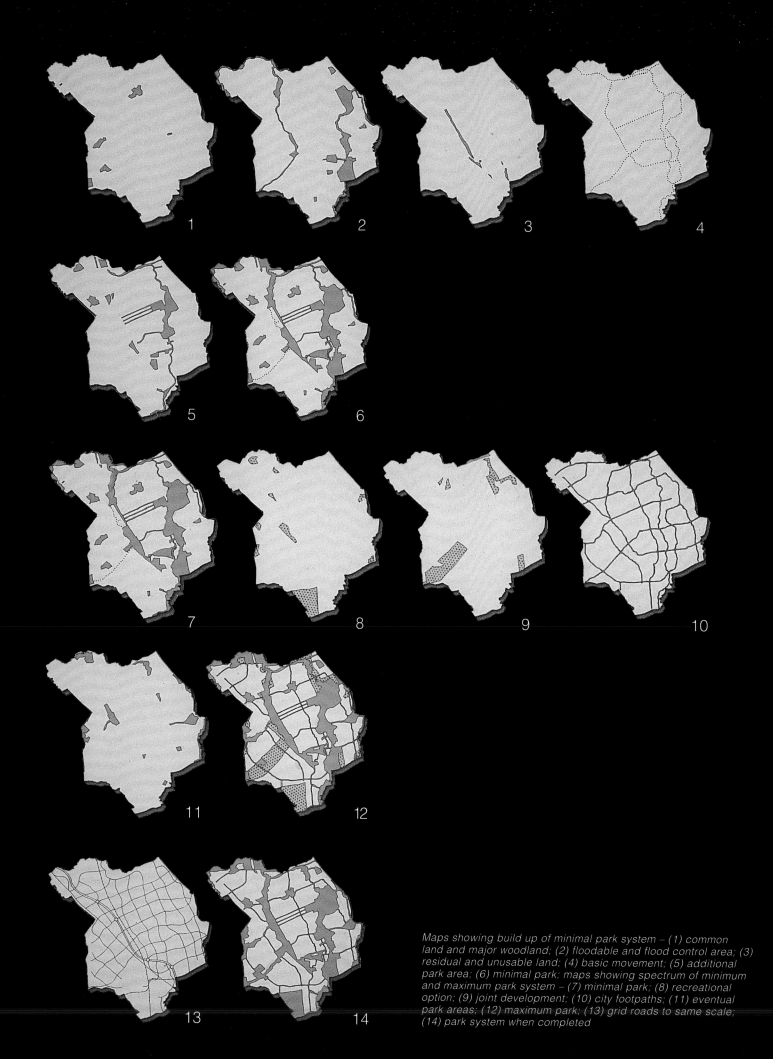

Maps showing build up of minimal park system – (1) common land and major woodland; (2) floodable and flood control area; (3) residual and unusable land; (4) basic movement; (5) additional park area; (6) minimal park; maps showing spectrum of minimum and maximum park system – (7) minimal park; (8) recreational option; (9) joint development; (10) city footpaths; (11) eventual park areas; (12) maximum park; (13) grid roads to same scale; (14) park system when completed

Footpaths and cycleways – the city has pioneered a comprehensive footpath and cycleway system to show for the first time on a citywide scale how travel for pedestrians and cyclists can be made convenient, safe and pleasant. The solution known as 'Redway' is an extensive network of footpaths/cycleways threaded through all areas of the city. Its most important feature is its complete separation from the city's main roads with the high level of safety that that brings. It is easily recognised by the red asphalt surfacing and is lit at 60 metre intervals. FROM ABOVE L TO R: Aerial view of redway system; canal towpath; village redway; city centre underpass; Springfield pedestrian edge; Great Linford redway, informal parking

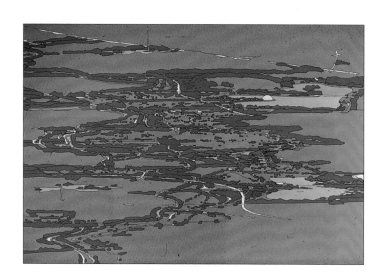

The linear park network in Milton Keynes forms a continuous mesh across the city whose basis is a series of movement patterns, generally along river valleys, for pedestrians, cyclists, horse-riders and water-borne transport. These routes form the structure of the park and were established early in the life of the city so that, no matter how prosperous or poor the future, a logical continuous system is assured, linking places of interest within the park and beyond the city boundaries. One of the Development Corporation's last acts was to set up a trust to administer the parks system throughout the next century. FROM ABOVE L TO R: toboganning, Willen Lake; canalside housing, MKDC; Waterside housing; village edge; linear parks; creating Willen Lake

Within the new city boundaries were 19 old communities of which 11 were small villages. Two thirds of these stand on the slightly higher land bordering the river valleys. Overall aims for each village in its new setting were based on an analysis of its existing character and possible surrounding land uses. FROM ABOVE L TO R: Model of Willen village plan; model of Great Linford village plan; model of Milton Keynes village plan; model of Woughton village plan; The Shenleys village plan; Great Linford, village implementation

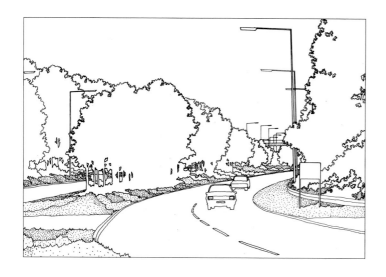

FROM ABOVE L TO R: Grid roads drawn in 1974; implemented grid road in 1994; hot air balloon over Loughton Bowl; model of Loughton Bowl; hot air balloon over teardrop lakes at Loughton

FROM ABOVE L TO R: Boule Court, Central Median, CMK; Bridge Link, CMK, MKDC (1976); Peace Pagoda overlooking Willen Lake; offices and infrastructure, CMK, MKDC (1973); lighting design, MKDC (1972); bus shelter prototype, MKDC (1974)

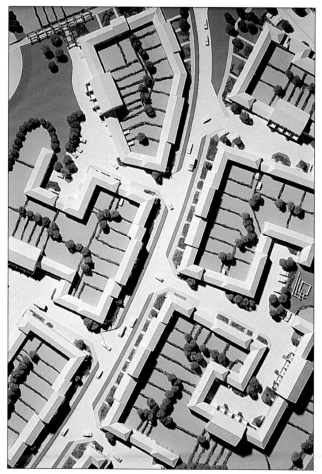

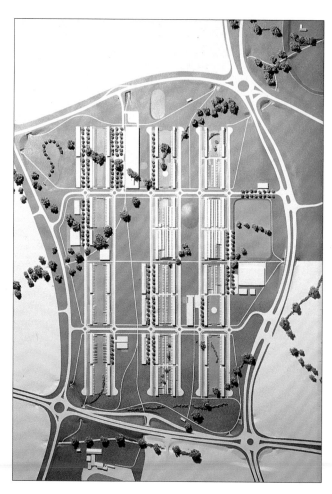

MARTIN RICHARDSON
HOUSING IN MILTON KEYNES

It was on the basis of my first commission in Milton Keynes, in 1973, that I set up my practice, and my tenth and final job there, designed in 1988, still awaits completion. So my view of the city is that of a participant. But I must also view it as an architect, not a journalist or sociologist. I can make no comment on the often significant direct, and indirect, effects of management. So, for better or worse, I judge it with my eyes.

I bring two criteria to bear, the enjoyment of the residents, manifest in their evident pleasure in – or abuse of – where they live, and architectural quality in its pure sense. The two don't always coincide. Where architectural ambitions, however perfect their geometry, however intriguing their social propositions, fail to work, then the architecture is, to my mind, diminished. At the other end of the scale, I cannot accept the grossest manifestations of builders' suburbia, however cherished by their owners.

After 20 years it is what has happened to the housing, what the residents have done, and how the fabric and landscape have matured or decayed that is so revealing. There is a range of responses. The right to buy has had problematical effects, where too often the insertion of plastic windows, fancy front doors, and even the veneering of the whole facade, seem to proclaim more conquest of ownership than love of habitat. As a general observation, I do believe that councils and corporations should have maintained a degree of control, as such estates as the Cadogan or Hampstead (Garden Suburb) have. It is tragic not only in Milton Keynes, but for example in the interwar cottage estates, to see destructive abuse of their often distinguished and quiet harmony. However, there are developments so beyond redemption that the attempt to make a home of your own in such a wilderness, by idiosyncratic transformation, seems legitimate. On the other hand there are places where the designer seems to have got it so right that the residents have either not felt the need to change, or have simply picked up the tune. Robust architecture and heavy landscape have proved their value.

The master planners of Milton Keynes, Llewellyn Davies, Weeks, Forestier-Walker and Bor, were in a position to learn from the whole experience of the New Towns in particular, and of post-war housing in general. They looked abroad, notably to the US, to sense what the future might hold. By

so doing they arrived at decisions that have in general proved mature and stood the test of time. They believed in pluralism – the offer of choice. It was accepted that dreams of the urban elite were not for the vast majority. Loose fit, plentiful space saved the city from the most unmanageable symptoms of high density. It was accepted that most people want to enjoy a car and that its proper accommodation takes space. And a belief in abundant and high quality landscape proved to be one of the city's major achievements.

The themes of the master planners were endorsed with enthusiasm and reinforced with quality by the executive designers, the Development Corporation led by Derek Walker, and its carefully selected consultants. Variety was seen as desirable not only to offer choice, but to respond to the more or less urban or suburban, flat or rolling, settled or contextless, nature of the parts of the city. Thus, the open abstraction of Netherfield, the restrained classicism of Fishermead, the pitched roofed, redbrick domesticity of Springfield, and the enclosed village texture of Eaglestone were initiated at the same time.

The ambitious launch of the early seventies, 3,000 dwellings a year, forced constraints on design. There were too few contractors, they tended to offer their preferred heavy or light systems, and they liked big sites. It was this that led to the great grid square developments, whose architects might have preferred sites of a tenth their size. It was this that led, for example, to Netherfield, conceived in brick, being realised in timber frame.

In the *AD*s of June 1973 and December 1975 Milton Keynes published images of its proposals, as they should appear then and in 20 years' time. That future is now, which makes it a good time to compare that flared-trousered, hopeful vision with the reality.

The polemical three – Coffee Hall (1973-76), Netherfield (1971-74), Bean Hill (1972-75) are as good a place to start as any. They represent the arrival and patronage of Derek Walker; his enrolment of architectural staff and private consultants of quality. They represent a rejection, or at least an addition, to the master planners' vision of a more relaxed, loosely spaced domestic environment. Their grid square scale proclaimed – why not? – 'this is the scale of the programme, of the time', and the straight lines were a represen-

ABOVE: Advertising suburbia; OPPOSITE FROM ABOVE L TO R: Oldbrook (MacCormac Jamieson Pritchard); Moot Hall at Great Holm, Edward Cullinan (1989); model of Neath Hill showing housing court, MKDC (1975); model of Netherfield showing grid square, MKDC (1972)

tation of production. Unexpressed may be that transparently macho desire on the part of ambitious architects for the extraordinarily long, straight, hard line, man's triumph over nature. In their neutral abstraction they also represent Melvin Webber's non-space urban realm, acknowledged by Walker as a key concept, where intimate local spaces, as an analogy of intimate local relations, were irrelevant in an imagined world of city wide if not global communication.

The ruthlessness of Netherfield is reinforced by its metal facades, a characteristic shared with Foster's Beanhill. The precedent of the Eames House, a metallic box, is misleading. When the environment itself is composed of such materials it seems to repel flora, fauna and human alike, magnetically to attract the detritus of living. Of Netherfield, Robert Maxwell wrote, 'If the houses are full of successful people, making their way in life, the image of the estate will be beneficent', but, he added, with prescience, 'If times get bad, if the consumer society breaks down, if deprivation sets in, things could be very different' (*Architect's Journal* 10/12/75).

For all that, I still remember the beauty of Beanhill's cornflower blue windows and black metal in its infancy, and the calm space of Netherfield still exhilarates. A whiff of the poetry of modernism survives. But it is in the city centre that the architecture of abstraction finds its appropriate fulfilment, where the most intimate engagement of building and people is uncalled for.

Next to, and contemporary with this trio stands Eaglestone (1972-75), Erskine's intricate web of instant villages. After the aristocratic lines and parkland of its neighbours, its miniature houses and spaces look crabbed and proletarian. Yet like it or not, this, I suspect, is much nearer the social and emotional reality of their occupants. And here it has to be remembered that the vision of the itinerant Milton Keynes voyeur is an unnatural one. Those who live there do not experience this tiresome iteration of minor domestic scale.

The central area housing, at Fishermead, its hard edged, flat roofed three-storey rationalist terraces in suave buff brick, along broad boulevards, enclosing wide squares, demonstrated what might have been hoped to have been a happy balance between urban order and domestic scale. But the cool purity of these districts is now lost under heavy pitched roofs. (I still do not understand why the flat roof remains such a problem in this country. In equally demanding climates abroad they still seem to happily build and maintain them.) But even in its prime, the dry abstraction of the central area housing was not unalloyed with a certain tedium. Its bland rigours in the hands of the zealous were symptomatic, I sometimes felt, of a disrespect for human sensibilities.

While the realisation of the central area was for the most part entrusted to the safe hands of the in-house architects, a number of privileged outsiders were admitted in the late seventies. Colquhoun and Miller's Oldbrook 2 (1979-82) is an essay in quiet neo-classicism distinguished not only for its architectural control, but by its wise tactics in material and detail. It survives in excellent shape, providing a convincingly habitable and urban environment. In Bradwell Common 1 (1978-81) I introduced a more intimate scale, variety and complexity, and an appeal to memory and the senses. In the very centre, an early scheme by Derek Walker in his private capacity, E1 2 (1977-80), simple, elegant yet domestic, in ochre brick and grey roofs, has stood the test of time with honours. Nearby is Wayland Tunley's E1 4 (1986-90), notable as a late, ambitious, but isolated attempt at high density private upmarket urban living.

Moving out from the inner sanctum of Central Milton Keynes, with its rectified grid and elite minimalism, we approach the more frankly relaxed, permissive, curvilinear, suburban, even rural outer areas, in effect the bulk of Milton Keynes. (The distinct character of this outer zone was ensured by its separate administration.) Neath Hill (1975-80) by Derek Walker and Wayland Tunley's in-house team, demonstrated the continuing soundness of the late Garden City approach, small groups of houses, in a liberating variety of formats, lining streets and enclosing carefully detailed cul-de-sacs, and always close to common green spaces. It is firmly based on the restrained and traditional use of traditional materials, but with an added, Scandinavian taste in stained timber. It was one of the last grid squares to be designed and built as an entity, and in spite of its highly crafted complexity suffers from the inevitable tedium of repetition. The most successful essay in this genre is perhaps the unassuming Hazelwood, Great Linford (1975-78), by Milton Keynes' in-house architects. Its quiet, sensible, normative style, that made unpolemical yet progressive use of traditional forms and materials has stood the test of time. It still feels right, appropriate for modestly off Britons to pursue their quiet lives, as it did in the 1970s. It avoids, equally, sentimental nostalgia and false futurism.

Richard MacCormac, at France Furlong (1975-77), and I in Hartley (1973-77), both nearby in Linford, also achieved something of this quality. Hartley and Hazelwood owe much to their carfree domestic environments, made possible by their grouped parking, a formula opposed by the conventional wisdom of the housing manager and estate agent, but which in the event proved no inhibition in the exercise of the right to buy; they were among the most desired developments.

The early seventies were in retrospect a happy moment. We had worked our way out of some of

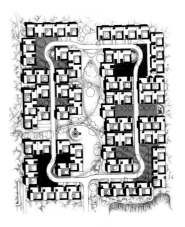

ABOVE: Site plan of Calverton End (Frost Nicholls); OPPOSITE FROM ABOVE L TO R: Fullers Slade (MKDC) 1971; Eaglestone (Ralph Erskine) 1972; Netherfield (MKDC) 1972; Calverton End, private housing, (Frost Nicholls) 1973; Canal side, Wayland Tunley, 1980; Milton Keynes village housing, private, (MKDC) 1972; cross sections through Netherfield three-storey terraces

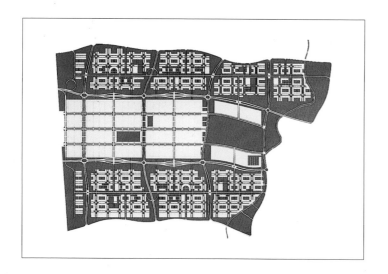

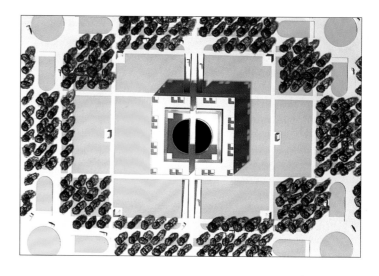

FROM ABOVE L TO R: Strategic plan for central housing for 30,000 people; model of apartment building in the central area; corner block at Fishermead; Springfield; street perspective of Fishermead; perspective of Fishermead Court

the fallacies of Modernism, yet, retaining something of its disciplines, were prepared to pick up what was relevant in traditional patterns and building methods, and achieved a sensible synthesis. This happy moment could not last. Attempts to add more richness, intricacy, detail and association resulted in a number of projects – for example MacCormac's Heelands 5/7 (1982), my own Bradwell Common 1 (1978-82), Cullinan's Downhead Park (1979) – which proved a little too self-consciously and unnecessarily elaborate. But by then rental housing was to come to a virtual halt in any case.

During the seventies a few small and distinguished groups of housing for sale had emerged. An early example was Frost Nicholl's Calverton End (1973-77) at Stony Stratford. MacCormac's Cottisford Crescent in Great Linford (1977), with overtones of Wright in its roofs and woodwork, is exceptional in its light elegance (1977). At Kindleton, Great Linford (1976-78) I suffered my first experience of diminishment at the hand of estate agents and builders. 'If 100 per cent of the public will buy two-storey, and even 60 per cent buy three-storey, why bother with it?' said the agent '. . . and more scaffolding said the builder . . . so lets drop it', they said. And details came out strangely transmuted.

In the eighties, apart from a few joint ownership schemes, private development took over. At first the Corporation endeavoured to exercise control in the form of a sometimes over fastidious, miniaturised beaux-arts urban design with a proliferation of small axes, symmetries and 'gateways'. Corporation control in the selection of architects gradually slackened, and eventually as houses became hard to sell, developers' license dominated. It is hard to find any really distinguished schemes of that period, even where better architects were used. During that time I myself built four developer projects. But the combined effect of a pressure to separate and individualise too many small houses on too little ground, and the absence of control over detail once the developer had made off with his planning permission, has meant that I have never wished to publish the results. On my latest visit I observed that my last scheme, which had achieved a degree of simple quality, but which had been suspended half complete over the recession, was underway again, but now using the standard developers' houses.

A tour through the great red/brown mass of developer housing in the outer areas is depressing. Here all the crassness of snobbery and nostalgia flourish in their tacky pathos. Persistently aiming above its station, the imagery always falls short of its target. The eagerness to proclaim individuality denies the benefits of a greater whole. What is doubly sad is that such housing, at least in the good times, was not short of purchasers. Never-

theless, the burgeoning fig leaves of the Corporation's landscape policy help sustain a relative degree of quality rare in the world outside.

Looking at this great 25 year experiment, I would suggest that the attributes of the more successful projects would seem to include the following:

- A good fit between what was offered and what was wanted. This may seem a truism, but the failure of awkward, unloved visions that haven't worked make the point.
- The evidence of the power of good design – where the layout as a whole is more than the sum of its parts, whose inevitable modesty then becomes less critical, The absence of this sense is the endemic weakness of developer housing.
- A certain substance and resilience that can absorb people's accessories and modifications. This means good borders between public and private, good enclosures to gardens or garages, strong detail.
- Layering, that transitional zone of eaves, porches, balconies and garden that mediates between public and private, hard and soft, outside and inside, and that can host nature.
- Closely related to the above is the use of natural material. It is surprising that still, as we approach the end of the twentieth century brick survives repeatedly as the most successful material. The metal panel, that symbol of modernism, so rarely works in practice.
- The successful accommodation of the car. The failure to do so can destroy an estate. The need to keep a cheap vehicle on the road tends to mean that the areas of severest need are also those most littered with vehicles in states of decay.
- Generous public landscape – and this is one of Milton Keynes' most enduring achievements. Its continuing maintenance, sadly is not always adequate.

To summarise, then, I believe that Milton Keynes was a good thing. Whatever one's views of New Towns, of low density living, of car dependency, Milton Keynes at least offers one exceptionally well worked out, and manifestly popular experiment. The country can afford one such alternative. It was built with optimism, conviction and enthusiasm. Diversity, quality and innovation were encouraged. The public realm was created with generosity.

For the last five years I have been designing, and continue to design, housing in Holland. There, they have not lost heart; progressiveness and optimism are alive and well among the producers and consumers of housing alike. It is hard to believe, after the cultural devastation of the last 15 years, that so relatively recently Milton Keynes enjoyed such optimism. What has happened? How can we turn things around?

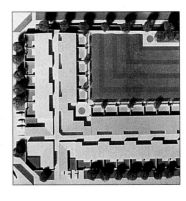

ABOVE: Springfield sheltered housing – model showing plan view; Jacoby indoor route

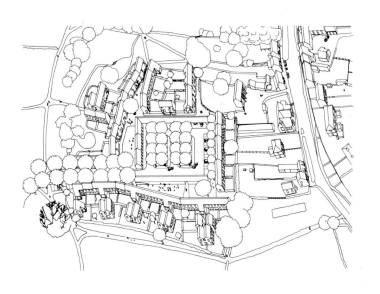

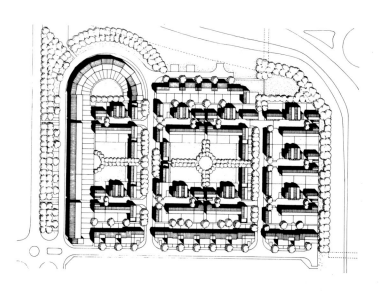

Martin Richardson at Milton Keynes: LEFT FROM ABOVE: Great Linford 5 (1973) – view from village; inner court (1973); site plan; RIGHT FROM ABOVE: Bradwell Common (1978) – elevations; housing; site plan

OPPOSITE FROM ABOVE: Martin Richardson – walkway in Great Linford; Bradwell Common Boulevard (1978)

39

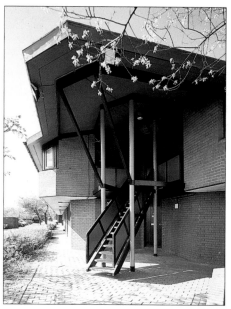

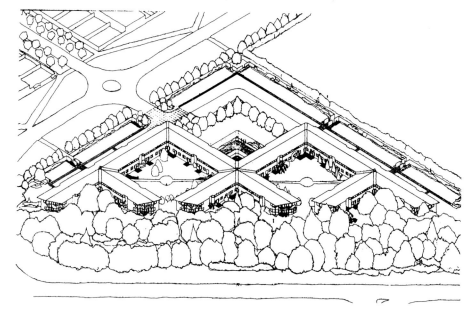

*FROM ABOVE L TO R: MacCormac Jamieson Pritchard –
Great Linford 12 (1976); Chapter House; axonometric
of Chapter House (1975)*

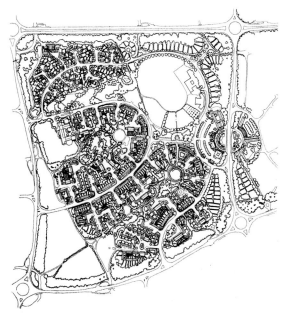

FROM ABOVE L TO R: Neath Hill, MKDC (1976) –
Local Centre; site plan; typical public housing

FROM ABOVE L TO R: E12 CMK, Derek Walker Associates (1978) – general views; view from shopping building; canalside at Great Linford, Stephen Gardiner (1975)

FROM ABOVE L TO R: Bradwell Common 2 – cycle path, Edward Cullinan (1979); site plan; Oldbrook, Colquhoun and Miller (1979)

STUART MOSSCROP
MAKING SENSE OF THE CENTRE

Twenty years on from the first phase of construction in Central Milton Keynes, the second major retail development is about to be launched – the biggest single move in the centre since the pre-recession flourish of new office floor space during the eighties. It is a new move, which presents both an opportunity and a threat: on one hand it is a chance to reaffirm the original goals of the plan for the city centre and redress the recent slump in quality and civic pride or, on the other, to disregard the lessons of the eighties in Central Milton Keynes and consolidate bad with worse. In any case 20 years is a convenient time for the first interim report on progress to date, and to renew hope for the future of the city centre in Milton Keynes.

Central Milton Keynes in 1994 carries much more than its fair share of bad buildings designed and built over the last decade – a dire and lasting epitaph to the Thatcher years of private gain at public cost. With few and notable exceptions there has been little or no architecture during this period, and civic design in some parts of the centre has been set back to the time when cave men were frightened by lightning. The contrast between the originating energy of the seventies and the cynical *laissez faire* of the eighties can be seen more clearly in the built environment of Central Milton Keynes than anywhere else in England. Clearly that is because the original progressive intent of Central Milton Keynes is still apparent and survives intact despite the battering of mediocrity sustained over the last ten years – the contrast between then and now is truly staggering.

The plan for Central Milton Keynes provided a structure of roads, boulevards, spaces and parks that would not rely, as earlier New Towns had, upon specific architectural set pieces to form the administrative, commercial and social core of the New Town. Designed primarily to serve citizens of Milton Keynes, it would also assume a regional significance because of its size and accessibility. It should be easy to get to, pleasurable to move through and around, and should accommodate a variety of built forms and transportation. Central Milton Keynes would not only meet the demand for conventional retail and commercial floor space but its generous land take and relaxed density would also provide a wide range of sites for those traditional city centre fringe uses unable to afford top prices for land or

buildings – essential to the choice and vitality of any decent centre. The public space, including roads and car parks, would be amply sized for future growth, trimmed with Cornish granite and decorated with trees, shrubs and flowers – the city centre would reflect the civilised and open spirit of the town itself. Above all, the centre was designed to accept and accommodate change without resort to major surgery or contortion, to meet the needs of its citizens of the time.

The physical infrastructure was committed in the early seventies and the first buildings to occupy the centre were enthusiastically designed by the Development Corporation as a demonstration of quality and statement of intent. The strength of the original concept and its physical infrastructure were to be tested sooner than thought in the market mania of the eighties.

For a retro trip through Central Milton Keynes property development in those crazy years, choose a dry day when the plane trees are in leaf and take a hike from Milton Keynes Central Station straight up Midsummer Boulevard. Across the public square is an elegant steel and granite bus station now desolated by the deregulation of public transport; to the north lies a bank or building society that should have known how to house itself better than it did, and straight ahead the boulevard is flanked by an extraordinary assortment of small and mostly hysterical office buildings shrieking their wares. Onward and upward to the topographical high point of Central Milton Keynes – the original meeting place of the Saxon hundred that once governed the area – but today crowned with an 'ecumenical facility' that would have Brunelleschi's ribs rattling. Across the way, the original city square to the west of the shopping building was never a success and deserved to be built upon – but the extension of the shopping building currently under construction on the site is an authentic 'carbuncle on the face of a well loved friend' falling disastrously between a self assured coda and a genuine extension of the original. Walk on past the only night marker of Central Milton Keynes from a distance – the red neoned Point – which together with a couple of burger and pizza joints constitutes the epicentre of 'after-hours' for a population of 200,000. Proceed through the open market until you clear the east end of the shopping building – which will be closed if it's later than 6.30pm – then sprint for

ABOVE: Shopping building, central open court, MKDC (1973-79); OPPOSITE: Concept of Central Milton Keynes 2000, MKDC (1972) by Jacoby

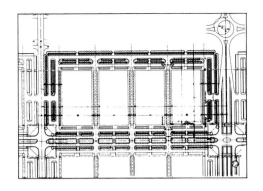
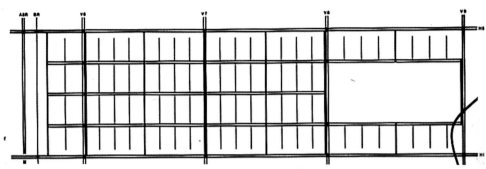

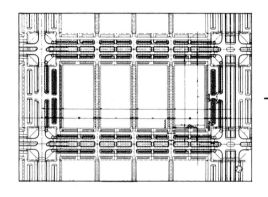
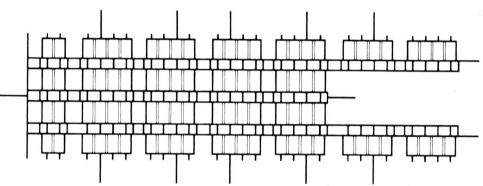

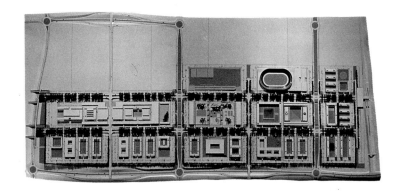

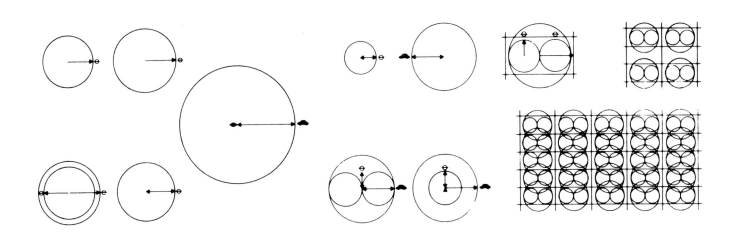

The design principle of the area plan for the centre provides a circulation system of service and access routes within which developments of different kinds and densities can take place, well landscaped with a palette of high quality and robust materials. The intention of the Central Milton Keynes area plan is to suggest a pattern of development which while not requiring the users to learn new or strange urban skills, has paradoxically offered them some of those urban delights, space, greenery, legibility and the opportunity for peace and quiet; in other words it will enable the public to experience and contribute to a rich environment free from the constraints often imposed by the very technologies with which man intended to liberate himself. FROM FROM ABOVE L TO R: Shopping building showing open square glazing (1978); model of Central Milton Keynes (1974); infrastructure, Central Milton Keynes, lanterns and seating; Porte Cochere by Jacoby; diagram of walking distances in Central Milton Keynes; OPPOSITE FROM ABOVE: Structure of inner block, Central Milton Keynes, MKDC, (1971); preferred vehicular net, Central Milton Keynes; outer block, Central Milton Keynes; pedestrian net; elevated servicing for shopping building; section through typical underpass; scale study of the shopping building on the Thames; section through typical boulevard

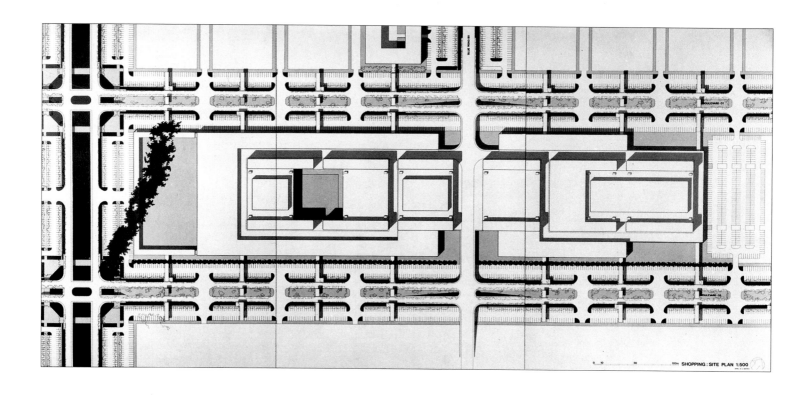

48

the serenity and quiet of Campbell Park to recover visual sensibility, reflect upon the architecture of late twentieth-century greed, and wonder where to catch a bus back to the station.

The decline in the quality of life in Central Milton Keynes can be reliably traced to the date at which POSTEL, the institutional investor in the shopping building, insisted upon closing the centre to the public at hours to suit its building management. The arcades and cross routes of the shopping area were designed as an integral part of the city centre street system and as such have no doors, so they had to be installed before they could be locked. But the building also contains two important public spaces in Central Milton Keynes, one an open garden court, beautifully revamped shortly after the original opening, and the other a well equipped covered space available for events other than turgid commercial promotions – neither of these spaces is now genuinely available to the public – they represent the ever growing, insidious privatisation of the public domain throughout the UK. Closing part of the city centre was quickly followed by a rationalisation of the public transport system for Central Milton Keynes whereby buses were routed for maximum cost effectiveness to the new operators, regardless of where

passengers wanted to go to or from. The new routes were so effective that the buses had to be slowed down by mounds of painted tarmac which were mistaken for pedestrian crossings until disclaimer signs appeared to warn people otherwise – municipal engineering wreaked vengeance upon profligate granite and unnecessary public spending. Miraculously the original horse chestnut and plane trees remain unscathed – though some have been eyed longingly by axe bearing traffic engineers, God forbid.

Central Milton Keynes has survived its first traumatic decade remarkably well and remains basically sound; recession forced a timely end to the madness of profit at any cost. This pause should be used to determine a return to enlightened patronage and creative decision making, the use of talented architects, engineers and designers of this generation may reboot the original drive and energy which will be needed to take the centre through its next ten years and beyond. Maybe some of those initial aspirations for a genuine mixed use centre can be realised, perhaps a useful modern public transport system will be established, early mistakes carefully rectified and civic pride restored – Milton Keynes and its people deserve at least that.

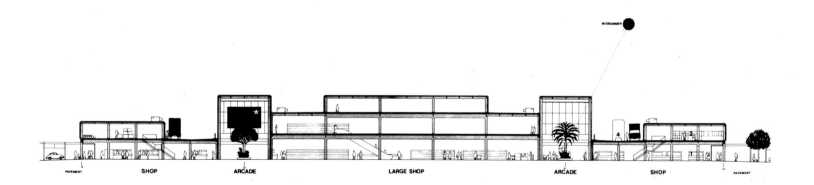

The first phase of the Shopping Building comprised 1,085,625 feet of gross lettable area. Carparking is arranged at ground level around the edges of development blocks immediately adjacent to the building. Vehicular service to the shops is by raised limited access road at first floor level. Shopping accommodation is divided into three bands separated by two 12 metre wide 14 metre high weather protected and naturally lit pedestrian arcades which are extensively planted. The central accommodation comprises the large department stores and contains two public squares one open and one covered. The bands on the north and south house unit shops, pubs and banks and have frontages on the street and arcade. The west end open market square which contains the only major mature tree belt in the city centre is now decimated and the square is being catastrophically developed, presumably as a reward for outstanding commercial success; it is a pity the current owners did not realise that the second phase was supposed to be at the eastern end of the centre. ABOVE: Typical cross section; OPPOSITE FROM ABOVE L TO R: Shopping Building, open court (1973); pub; site plan; open square at night; original model of Shopping Building

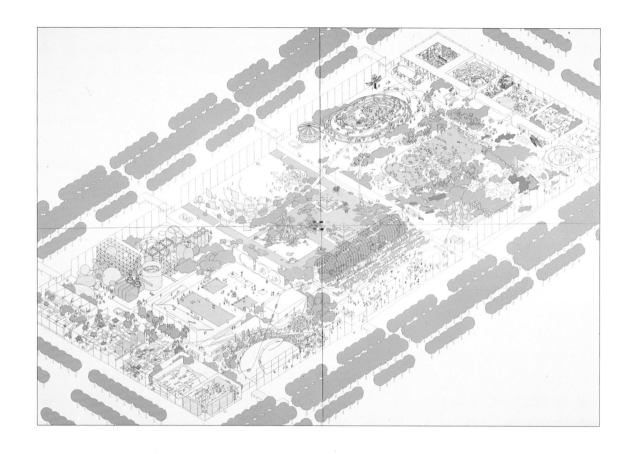

FROM ABOVE: City Club Mark 11, MKDC (1974-76);
City Stadium Mark 1, MKDC (1974)

One of the most salutary lessons of the eighties is that in surburban Britain the bottom line rules. Classic hopes for the city's leisure packages were dashed with the demise of the City Club after three bites at funding, a rebuff for the Wonderworld Group, and the demise of the Branson package which led the corporation into the ever willing hands of Britain's longest running horror show: the standard leisure package, as unimaginative as it is vulgar. The

overtures of Luton Town were never consummated and the stadium and sports club for Milton Keynes are available only in diminished form as the centre for national field hockey. FROM ABOVE LEFT: What we wanted: MOMA Sculpture Garden, New York, Philip Johnson; Kowloon Park, Hong Kong, Derek Walker Associates; Willis Faber, Ipswich, Foster Associates; FROM ABOVE RIGHT: What we got: Ecumenical Centre; The Point; speculative potboilers

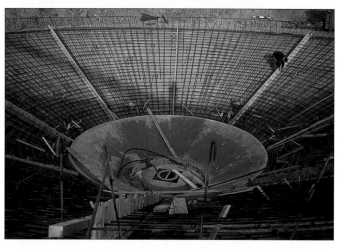

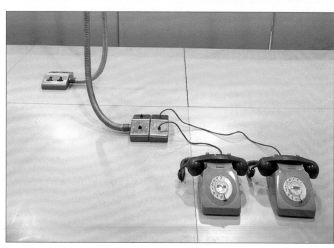

DEREK WALKER
INDUSTRIAL AND COMMERCIAL BUILDINGS

Reduced to the simplest equation, new towns are about jobs and homes. The strategic plan for the South East made Milton Keynes a major growth point in the region with the task of providing jobs and houses for 150,000 newcomers by the early 1990s. Employment opportunities were the key to meeting this target. A variety of jobs were to be provided and market forces determined the final manufacturing structure. Current indicators confirm the initial prediction that incoming industry would be dominated by the three engineering SIC orders, with printing and publishing and all major distributive industries playing an important role.

Apart from the quantity and quality of new jobs provided, the City had a series of continuing objectives. These included provision of an attractive working environment, a design service for industrialists building their own plants, and rental accommodation for immediate occupation, which had to be flexible in use and capable of accepting a wide range of activities and occupiers.

One of the key projects to set the precedent for industrial and commercial development was the Development Corporation's redesign of the Sewage Works (1970) with its formal landscape setting, organised geometries and simple detailing techniques which provided a template for the industry groups in establishing a pattern of development where workspaces could be enhanced by ordered planning and the provision of a major infrastructure of planting.

Research at Milton Keynes and elsewhere has shown that an industrial building should rarely be closely tailored to the industrialist's particular needs during the initial stages. Changes in process and technique are frequent. A new machine may radically alter production methods or layout. A company may expand out of its building and another move in. To adapt to changes of process and product the building's shell must be capable of accommodating a wide variety of products and machinery sizes and loadings. Services have to be easily changed and upgraded.

The Development Corporation's mandate in 1970 was to respond to a probable demand for some 50,000 square metres of industrial floor space each year, and to cope with the rapid growth we produced a short and a long term strategy. In the long term we hoped to produce an elegant building system flexible enough to deal with most industrial needs.

The rationalisation of components and procedures saves time and money, design and construction, a major advantage to both the client and developer. By standardising a generous shell which can be tuned as required, obsolescence is reduced to a negligible level.

The System Building for Industry did not attempt to cater for all industrial activities, some are too specialised for an off the peg solution. However it provided speed, performance and flexibility for the majority of industry which has come to the city.

Development and testing of a new system was a 12 month programme and the short term strategy as an interim measure ensured that immediate needs were met for factory space by conventional constructional structural methods with variation and adjustments in skin techniques, coupled with basic exercises in maximum site coverage. This approach, together with a generous landscape policy for all our industrial parks was fundamental, whichever system was used.

The full potential of SBI was never fully realised because it was never possible to fully rationalise design tendering and production procedures. Serial contracting was impossible with an industrial development programme that could be erratic and dynamic simultaneously. This problem, coupled with erratic building costs in an inflationary period, baulked a very earnestly researched system that offered such a sensible and simplified service to the incoming industrialists.

Alongside these strategies ran a parallel development for factory and commercial buildings. A number of manufacturers leased sites and used their own architects or designers under tight development control pertinent to the industrial park and a number of instant marriages were arranged between well known architects and industrialists.

The greatest disappointment in the early years was the aborting of five major complexes designed respectively by James Stirling and Partner, Foster Associates, YRM, Jack Bonningon and Farrell Grimshaw. The city's high standard of performance in industrial and commercial buildings tends to be in the low cost speculative area. The total picture would be so much richer if these projects had materialised.

OPPOSITE FROM ABOVE L TO R: Sewage works, MKDC (1970) – model; detail of facade; construction in progress; Sherwood House – view of facade; study model; office interiors; flexible services; prototype industrial units at Water Eaton, MKDC (1970) – prototype SBI

53

FROM ABOVE L TO R: SBI System, Wavendon
Prototype, MKDC (1970) – general view of cladding
system 1; typical glazed wall; interior showing
mezzanine; interior showing flexible services

*FROM ABOVE L TO R: Kiln Farm, MKDC (1971) – SBI
system at Wavendon; glazing; Steinberg/Butte Knit
SBI (1973); detail of up-and-over door*

FROM ABOVE L TO R: Mixed development at Cofferidge Close,
Stony Stratford, MKDC (1972); the creation of new enterprises, MKDC
(1973); Cofferidge Close Arcade; small units in Linford (1978)

*ABOVE: SBI, Scicon Kiln Farm, MKDC (1972) – exterior and interior;
BELOW FROM L TO R: Blakelands speculative units, MKDC (1978);
C14 speculative offices, Central Milton Keynes, MKDC (1974)*

DEREK WALKER
UNBUILT MILTON KEYNES

New city building is remarkably like a post-mortem on a fishing trip, the most significant fish are the ones that got away. Milton Keynes has lost – through bad luck, over optimism, international recession, and timidity – a number of projects that would have helped make the city beautiful, increase civic pride and, perhaps more important, lead to exceptional job opportunities.

At the outset of development the city had its share of luck when the Open University located itself in the city, adjacent to the Linear Park at Walton between Simpson and Milton Keynes Village. Equally important was the implementation of the Shopping Building which in its early years attracted shoppers from as far afield as Cardiff and Carlisle. The trick was always to consolidate these twin poles of culture and commercial success. The loss of Jim Stirling's sublime scheme for Olivetti on the brink of implementation and the subsequent demise of Stirling and Wilford's British Telecom Headquarters for political reasons deprived the city of two elegant campus solutions that provided much more than a place of employment. Each took a sector of the city and responded to a developed landscape. Each complex, set in generous public spaces, responded to the Corporation's policies on public accessibility. Similarly Norman Foster's German Car Centre scheme adjacent to Linford Wood provided Linford with a unique ecological solution which the subsequent piecemeal developments have not. Foster's solution provided public access, maintenance and enhancement to the wood, underwritten by the industrialist. It was one of Foster's best researched, commercial and industrial projects following on from Willis Faber and IBM and had all the promise of a classic intervention.

Internally one catastrophic loss was the centrepiece of the Linear Park: the Willen Lake project, where a generously landscaped low-rise covered development supported the public leisure facilities. They included a pub overlooking the lake, a yacht club, hotel, restaurants and public areas for concerts and promenading – the inserts of a water organ and performance amphitheatre was a Hollywood Bowl come to Milton Keynes. Its demise left the area with a less ambitious strategy which culminated in the early eighties with an indifferent development of offices and leisure facilities which do little to enhance the heavily landscaped edge of the man-made lake. The northern section, however, retains a much more acceptable persona with an axial composition linking the Peace Pagoda with a ground level maze and Robert Hooke's lovely church in Willen Village. Another loss was the inability of the city to build on the obvious opportunity offered by the central area housing squares and the corner blocks. It had long been a wish of the architectural and social development teams to populate these areas close to the centre with modern commercial inserts, shops, professional offices, garden centres, community group buildings, kindergartens and gymnasia. The richness that this would have given to the central area is demonstrated in the Jacoby drawing. The development of community workshops also lost its impact in the eighties and the component design scheme in steel and glass was never implemented, nor was the television aerial for the city, elegantly designed by the infrastructure group in collaboration with Tony Hunt. Even Minale Tattersfield's graphic solution for citywide signing was jettisoned for a more conventional solution which, though very cleverly designed, never quite recaptured the slightly anarchic and ironic view that Brian Tattersfield always brings to his graphic solutions.

Perhaps the greatest personal loss were those projects developed by Andrew Mahaddie and members of my own practice. The City Park and two versions of the City Club designed in-house, the City Club Mark III and the Sculpture Park designed by my practice: the City Park was to me one of the more lyrical and impressive designs carried out within the corporation, its linkages down to the canal and Willen Lake provided such a rich assemblage of elements: a tree lined boating lake with seats designed in collaboration with local schools; a viewing cone eroded to provide sensory chambers and shelters; cascading water courses linked to a reflecting pool that assembled a whole series of party tricks from Frankenstein fog to step sensitive lighting devices and children's animation. The park edge contained a valley garden with scented planting for the blind, glass bridges, sculpture gardens, and a myriad of jogging trails and quiet walks.

In a sense poetry also dictated the original brief for a City Club. The two Fauik brothers who had

OPPOSITE: Theme Park, Bletchley Brick Pits Area, MKDC (1974) scheduled for the Millennium

organised the Isle of Wight Pop Festival were the promoters of an approach to leisure which had more in common with Joan Littlewood's Potteries Think Belt than the conventional leisure package – it contained a cultural centre, galleries, concert hall, theatre, cinemas, shopping, street theatre, radio and television studios, sports facilities and wavepool in a richly planted landscape setting. It would have provided the city with a real foil for the shopping building and a unique combination of activity under one roof. A covered stadium was also developed capable of housing pop concerts, league soccer, exhibitions and conference areas. The hope stayed alive long enough for us to pursue the concept with another client in moderated form in 1977, but that and a parallel exercise by Norman Foster with Granada came to nothing, leaving conventional morality in leisure the winner over imagination, underlining the story of Britain in the eighties.

Culturally the city had always been innovative. The workshops, Stantonbury theatre, Bletchley Leisure Centre, local activity groups, artists, performers and a multiplicity of organisations covering dance, theatre and music had flourished on lean pickings and public demand, but the most innovative option made available to the Corporation in 1977 was the development in the City Centre Park of an International Sculpture Park backed by Henry Moore, Phillip King, Anthony Caro and many other British sculptors. The concept had such promise – goodwill from a generous artistic community but very little support from central government. The designs were taken to a developed stage where phased development was possible but the axe fell in 1979 at the onset of the great Thatcher crusade. Will real patronage ever return to provide the city with the gems of quality and cultural stimulus that make a city memorable?

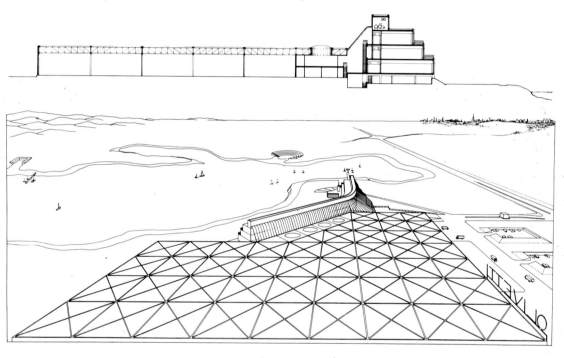

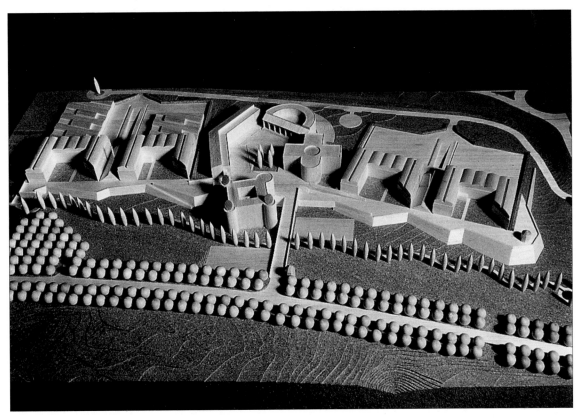

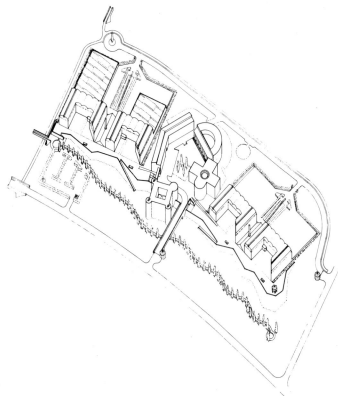

Olivetti Headquarters, James Stirling and Partner (1971) – this design was to be the focal point of a newly landscaped park, the Head Office overlooking a lake, stores and workshop buildings, screening them from the grid road. A glazed concourse provided gallery access to office and warehouse accommodation and to the car parks beyond. The conference centre is suspended above the main entrance. A worldwide building freeze imposed by Olivetti prevented the building going ahead and equally unfortunate for Stirling and Wilford was the cancellation of the British Telecom project through staff pressure and financial constraints imposed by the move from London. It is particularly sad to lose two elegant solutions particularly as it leaves the city without a building by Stirling and Wilford. FROM ABOVE: British Telecom Headquarters – model of complex; site axonometric (1984); OPPOSITE FROM ABOVE: Olivetti Headquarters – section through warehouse and office; aerial perspective of complex; model of entrance area

A keenly anticipated development was Foster's complex for the car dealer Thames Tilling. The scheme for Linford Wood was significant for the enlightenment brief prepared by Foster and his clients allowing public access to the wood. The campus development was beautifully conceived but aborted when Tillings sold on their concessions – the tragedy for the city was that sometime later Lonrho developed their concession for VW/Audi on another site as a package deal. Equally disappointing was the loss of the Entertainment and Leisure Centre which would have been perhaps too radical for Granada. The complex was contained in a 50x75 metre covered lightweight space with a perimeter frame 15 metres high for large-scale advertising and supergraphics. The facility would have contained a bingo club, a multiscreen cinema, disco, squash courts, amusements and restaurants; FROM ABOVE L TO R: German Car Centre, Linford Wood (1974) – Mercedes sector overlooking the woods; Audi sector; VW sector; OPPOSITE FROM ABOVE: Granada Leisure Centre (1979) – model; detail of the facade

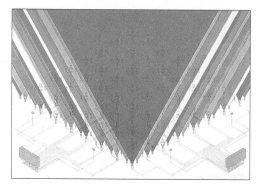

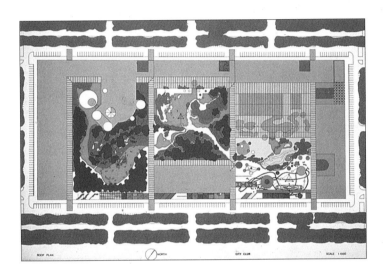

ABOVE FROM L TO R: City Club Mark I, MKDC (1972) – perspective of garden court and wave pool; indoor sports hall; City Club Mark III, Derek Walker Associates (1977) – site plan; theatre enclave; facade study; wave pool; OPPOSITE FROM ABOVE L TO R: Willen Lake development, MKDC – aerial view (1992); drawing of pub promon- tory by Jacoby (1972); model showing development plan (1975); pub interior; study for water organ; yacht club by Jacoby; model of water organ; Cofferidge Office Court; summer Sundays 1993; low- rise offices

Telephone

Cycle Track

Police

Golf

Picnic Area

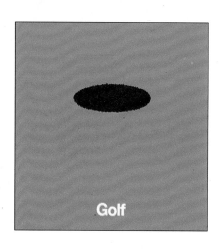

Bletchley Station

Wildlife Reserve

River

Secondary School

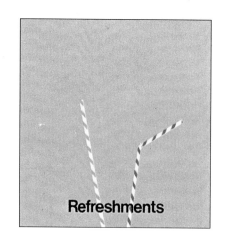

Refreshments

Sports Area

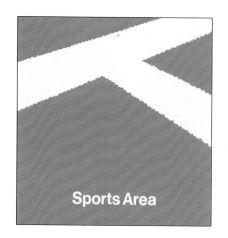

66

Even more infuriating than missing things you haven't got is getting substandard products when excellent ones have been rejected, or not using existing spaces imaginatively. A study for Central Area Housing suggested multi commercial and community uses in the pedestrian squares; it was not developed. The covered square in the shopping centre lacks a perimeter edge of activity throughout the day and evening. The workshop success was not consolidated and those wonderful adult centres have not been built in the profu-

sion first envisaged. Finally instead of the handsome central television aerial developed by the Development Corporation and Tony Hunt we are left with a limp apology. FROM ABOVE L TO R: Television aerial for the city, MKDC/Tony Hunt (1975); central area housing (1973) commercial and social inserts; Middleton Hall Shopping Building (1972-77), MKDC airshow; OPPOSITE: Minale Tattersfield signing package (1975)

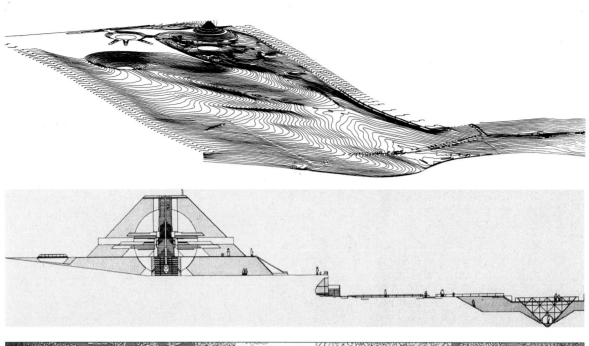

It was hoped that the City Parks illustrated here would be developed through the charity of city contractors, public participation, utilisation of adjacent engineering budgets, and occasional site development windfalls. A start was made but hard times and a design shift in the late seventies conspired to block the proposal. Though a pleasant park has developed, the richness of this proposal has been lost and another city landmark will not be realised. FROM ABOVE L TO R: Axonometric; section through the cone; boating lake and seating area; perspective view of cone and water carpet; OPPOSITE: Derek Walker Associates developed a proposal for the Milton Keynes Foundation for an International Sculpture Park to be located on the edge of the city park. It

proposed a centre of excellence for sculpture in the UK together with studio and educational facilities for artists and local children. The building form consists of a series of plateaued courts generated from a continuous ramp which links internal galleries with large outdoor courts and glades. The ramped form offered crucial phasing options, Henry Moore as president elect had offered a wide selection of his pieces on permanent loan, as had many other of his internationally known colleagues, but still government would not back the project and another fine facility was lost. FROM ABOVE L TO R: Perspectives showing: ramp through building; typical gallery; outdoor court; outdoor glade; transitional gallery; site plan; model of complete Sculpture Park Building

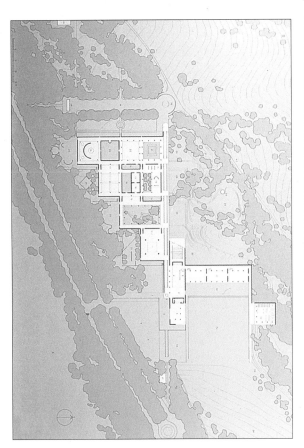

MICHAEL BRETT
THE VIEW FROM GREAT LINFORD

No doubt ordinary residents of Leeds, Bristol and Buffalo, New York, seldom reflect on the origins, character and mechanics of the cities in which they live. Still less are they likely to wonder whether they live in cities at all. But questions like these are hard to avoid at Milton Keynes. If the difference between linear and cyclical time signals one of many obvious distinctions between urban and rural life, at Milton Keynes they are both present in constant counterpoint. It is hard to avoid the sensation of living in a mechanism, a project forever in a state of introspective mobility where the future is composed of programmes and objectives, the past always at hand in the vestiges of ancient meadows and hedgerows that pop up through new paving and landscape, and the present an unending application of human and mechanical energy to the soil.

This has been an instructive background to the work of the Derek Walker Associates planning team which has operated from Great Linford since the practice was re-formed in 1976. Watching the new city grow around us has helped both to form and sustain many of the principles which underpin the practice's work.

The first of these emphasises the central role of the route system – the roads, transitways and footways – as the fundamental organising framework for all urban structures. The route system provides the basis both for the disposition of the city's functional areas, and for the generic assembly of urban spaces which give the city its visual language and character. In the low density environment of Milton Keynes we have become particularly interested in the use of landscape as an organising element both of urban space and of urban structure.

Our second key principle is concerned with the extreme uncertainty with which the planner must approach his work, particularly the larger and longer term project. New concepts are emerging as our culture shifts gradually from a Newtonian to a 'chaotic' or quantum view of fundamental physical structures. 'Chaotic systems', write Zohar and Marshall in their recent book, *The Quantum Society*, 'are not really indeterminate, they are just astoundingly complex', but they go on to discuss the potential of quantum theory to provide a mirror to various mental and social processes. In this view the importance of interactions within the urban system in confirming both the 'meaning' and 'utility' of the city would be underlined, but so would the futility of any attempt to 'model' such interactions, at least in the sense used by urban planners, particularly in an urban situation which is evolving over time. The urban planner, like the designer of any other mechanism, must of course proceed from some understanding of both purpose and process in the city. We believe that in much urban planning this understanding can be no more than approximate and that whatever the initial intentions it is impossible to exaggerate the extent to which urban structures have to be designed to accommodate unpredictable outcomes.

This was foremost in our minds when in 1984 we were asked to do some work for the industrial city of Jubail on the eastern seaboard of Saudi Arabia. Having completed earlier proposals for Haii Jalmudah, a district in the north-east part of the city, we were asked by the Royal Commission to participate in the complete revision of the plan for that part of the city not already committed to construction. It soon became clear, as we debated the issues in our roaring air-conditioned hut in the desert, that high on the list of factors we would need to consider was the infinitely complex process of implementation on which the vast army of foreign specialists employed by the government was already engaged. At the 'front line' we found in progress an unending round of budgeting, land allocation, survey and construction, design and re-design, re-scheduling of work and priorities, and re-allocation of resources. Issues of 'process', it seemed to us, were more important in some ways than issues of 'structure' and the fact that the existing plan had collapsed under the strain tended to support this view. We proposed that the plan be reorganised on a 'modular' basis. The completely flat terrain seemed to provide an opportunity to deploy the geometry of the route grid to something approaching its complete logical expression and to exploit the adaptability of the grid as a modular planning tool, giving the developer the opportunity to reorganise land uses within the route matrix as priorities changed. The sequence of drawings which illustrates the Jubail proposals was a manual for the assembly of the urban route network and the generic system of spaces which the network represents. We are not looking at the

LEFT: Kowloon Park, Hong Kong, Derek Walker Associates (1989)

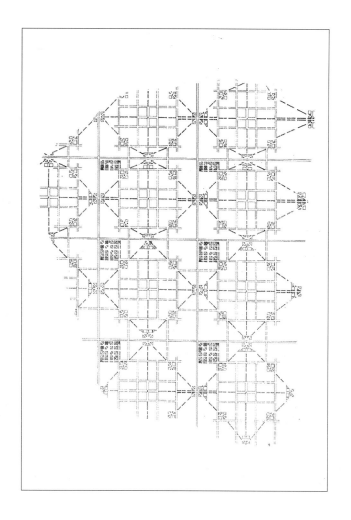

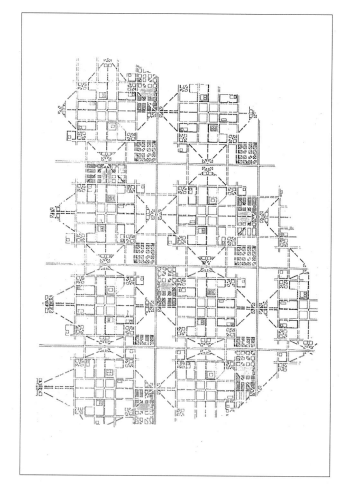

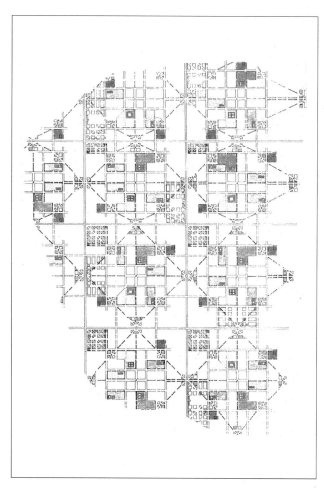

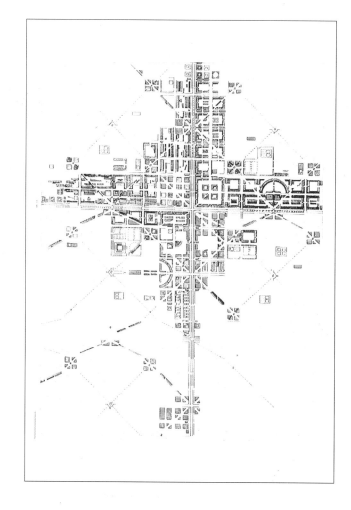

subdivision of the primary elements in a series of 'hierarchies'. On the contrary, the network is assembled by the overlay of elements which are of more or less equal status in spatial terms. Nor are we looking, in the first instance, at functional relationships within the urban system. The network assembles to provide a number of acceptable alternatives and choices for the distribution of functions; local centres, parks, schools, service areas can appear, disappear and reappear according to the rules of the game. Each can be replaced by housing clusters at a variety of densities. At Jubail the route structure itself was to some extent predetermined which had both advantages and disadvantages.

At Rotterdam in 1983 the team was asked to participate in a limited competition to generate ideas for the re-assembly of a working community in a run-down docks area known as Kop van Zuid on the south-east edge of the commercial centre and the Nieuwe Maas. The brief called for industrial regeneration, around 9,000 new homes, schools and commercial facilities.

If the Jubail proposals represented the construction of a system of urban geometry on an almost empty canvas, the need in Rotterdam was to explore the structural subtleties of an existing city of great age and character. A route system would be teased out of the existing grain of the city as if it were already there. Our exploration of the texture of the city revealed the old drainage channels or singels, usually in grid formation, mirrors to the Dutch sky, bridges, grassy banks and avenues of poplars; and pairs of straight roads, regular cross-routes forming blocks of about 240x50 metres (or 15-20 frontages in length), with the scale and consistency of the housing block providing the definition of a primarily linear spatial framework.

From these clues we devised a route structure with three levels, each with a distinct but complementary role. At the primary level structural continuity is achieved with three new cross-routes bridging Binnenhaven and Spoortweghaven and extending the existing main routes east and west to provide a distribution framework and tie the area back to the city's primary route structure. At the secondary level we sought textural consistency and a tensile framework to pull together scattered development areas by introducing the single and cross-route theme, resulting in promenades, avenues and water, a polished perspective of light and shade under bridges, twin avenues of broad-leaved trees, gardens, hedges and two twin lane roads. Finally we added the third layer, the system of walkways and cycle routes which break the network down to small corners, courts and enclosures rich with textured surfaces, seats, children's play frames, flower stalls, shelters and awnings. In descending levels of the framework we proceeded from an emphasis on the ordering characteristics of the geometry to a process of fragmentation in which the potential of the structure for achieving variations and complexities is revealed. At every level the role of the structure in ordering and unifying space is perceptible and all spaces within the matrix are of equal status. There are no hierarchies.

In 1992 we were in Japan preparing a master plan for the development of a New Town on a 250 hectare site of mixed farmland and woodland at Ushiku, about 45 kilometres north-east of Tokyo city centre and 27 kilometres from Narita airport on the Joban railway line. Almost everything about the scheme was in marked contrast to our familiar Milton Keynes back garden: the exceptional natural beauty of the site, the incredible residential densities proposed by the developer – 15,000 dwellings at 50 to the acre gross – and the high average household sizes. But our priorities remained the same, the development of a rational route structure and despite the densities, the deployment to their maximum advantage of the natural qualities of the site.

Housing clusters in towers and terraces together with their supporting facilities are placed on the flat hilltops where cool breezes alleviate the humidity of the hot summers, retaining the enclosed valleys for recreation, sports and community facilities. The wooded hillsides between housing and valley bottoms are preserved.

Intended primarily as a commuter town with little more than internal service employment, the main purpose of the community's route system is to link the housing clusters to a new station and regional commercial centre on the Joban line. This is achieved by means of a single main loop and cross route combining road and transit traffic and linking all the clusters, local centres and community facilities to the regional centre.

Ushiku is intended to be implemented in stages as a single major operation and there is little of the fuzziness in the proposals which would attend the uncertainties of long-term forecasting.

In 1991 we were successful in an international competition for Star Site, the gateway to Birmingham on the M6 to be developed as a business and cultural centre which would remain active and alive after business hours. Here the route structure is based on parallel distributor roads defining a central landscaped mall flanked by low to medium rise office buildings. At the focus of the mall, astride the Grand Union Canal which traverses the site, is the Central Arena, a complex of high rise office towers, a four star hotel, speciality retail, cultural and leisure facilities. Star Site is seen as an urban composition, available, accessible and comprehensible to employees and visitors. Despite the immense parking requirement – 12,500 spaces – all the main activities to which the public have access are at ground level which is given to streets, spaces, landscape and

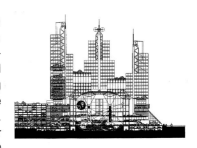

ABOVE: Central Arena at Star Site, Birmingham, Derek Walker Associates (1991); OPPOSITE: Urban geometry for the New City of Jubail, Saudi Arabia, Derek Walker Associates, Brett, Barker, Walker (1980) – network assemblies for distribution of functions

73

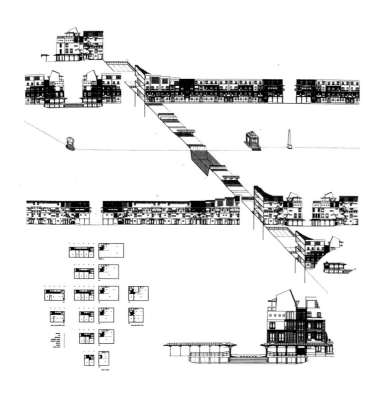

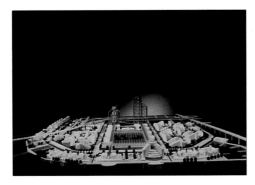

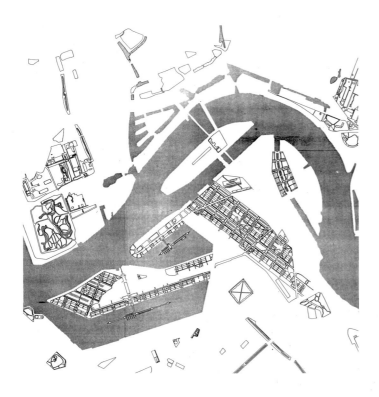

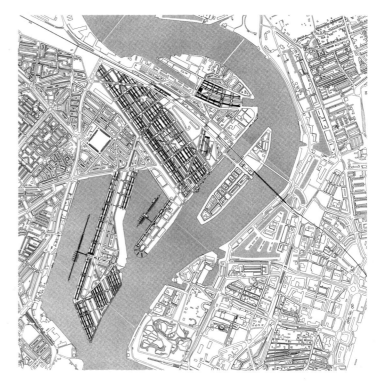

water. Parking and servicing are above ground or at basement level.

In the mid1980s the team was asked to carry out two commissions for clients in the United States. Again, contrast and paradox were the order of the day, and again, landscape and the route structure were the predominant themes. We were asked to prepare proposals for the development of Telluride, a nineteenth-century gold mining town 8,000 feet up in Colorado's San Juan Mountains, a successful ski resort since the mid-1960s. There was extreme local sensitivity to the form and content of any new development in the valley, so after a painstaking visual, environmental, and ecological appraisal had been carried out with the cooperation of local groups, landscape and the immense scale of the surrounding terrain were allowed to take over. Both the new route system and the 7,000 new bed spaces in a range of resorts, condominiums and lakeside hotels were sited in scattered locations and as far as possible 'lost' in the surrounding wilderness.

Meanwhile we were invited to prepare a master plan for Commodores Point, a tract of 150 acres of flat riverfront land between two high level road bridges about a mile east of the downtown business centre of Jacksonville, Florida. With good access and visibility, exceptional river views to the south and east and nearly 6,000 linear feet of waterfront, Commodores Point provided an opportunity for a major mixed-use development including a variety of integrated commercial, retail, residential, civic and tourist oriented projects, to be completed in three phases. At the core of the site there were 600,000 square feet of retailing combined with a children's adventure park, anchored by three department stores, a hotel and office tower. A mile of riverside development included two boat marinas, restaurants, clubs, shops and apartments, as well as a museum/art gallery for the city. To tie all this together, the route system consisted of a straightforward extension into the area of two main east-west downtown streets, Adams and Duval, linked by a new loop road serving waterfront development.

The 1980s also saw the completion of commissions in the Far East and Europe. In Hong Kong the team was asked by the Royal Hong Kong Jockey Club and Urban Council to prepare a master plan for the complete renewal of Kowloon Park, a traditional 23 hectare urban park in the busy Tsim Sha Tsui section of Kowloon. The project included the construction of a major sports facility comprising indoor sports halls and a swimming complex including an Olympic standard competition pool as well as the complete renewal of the park itself.

Features incorporated into the new park, planned around a strong north-south axis leading to the sports centre on Austin Road, include an outdoor arena and piazza, children's adventure playground, viewing cone, landmark, water gardens, sculpture garden, Chinese garden, aviary, history museum, scent garden and maze. The park and centre opened to the public in 1989.

Earlier, back in Rotterdam, we had been commissioned to prepare plans and designs for the renewal of the Lijnbaan, a pioneering traffic-free shopping centre in the heart of the city completed by Broek en Bakema in 1953. After 30 years the centre was in serious physical decay and there had been a marked deterioration in trading performance. The solutions proposed amounted to a radical programme of commercial, physical and management reconstruction. New anchors at the north and south ends of the pedestrian 'spine' were introduced, as well as a new trading and circulation level at the first floor, 'gateways' and improved vertical circulation, and a trading zone policy including a central zone for exhibitions, entertainments and displays. The entire pedestrian core of the development was to be covered with a lightweight translucent canopy designed by Buro Happold, with improved lighting, signs and street furniture. This project's exposure in Holland led to work on the old Heineken brewery site in Amsterdam – the Pipj – as a community development for the district.

The planning team is currently busy in Leeds on the development of Clarence Dock completed to serve the city at the head of navigation on the River Aire in 1843. This followed the Trustees of the Royal Armouries' announcement in June 1991 that the greater part of the unique collection of arms and armour would move to the site from its traditional home at the Tower of London. Derek Walker Associates won the competition to prepare the master plan for the 37 acre site, sponsored by Leeds Development Corporation, and were subsequently asked by the Trustees to design the museum (currently under construction) and the interior displays.

The site for the museum itself is a promontory between Clarence Dock and the River Aire adjacent to the river lock and Leeds Weir. In this position the six storey building has a dominant and pivotal relationship with the river, the dock and other development within the dock area. The theory of a pedantically dictated environment is historical nostalgia. The key to high design standards is to continue to emphasise two main issues: good ideas and good people. Certainly it is only the most persuasive and knowledgeable design controllers who can fight the battle with the British private developer who has yet to offer convincing evidence of quality performance in our cities.

OPPOSITE FROM ABOVE L TO R: Housing at Kop van Zuid, Rotterdam, Derek Walker and Peter Barker (1983); model showing typical block in the regeneration of Dockland, Jacksonville, Florida, Derek Walker and Associates; Kop van Zuid – development model; existing site; model from river frontage; Lower Kop van Zuid, detail of site plan; site plan

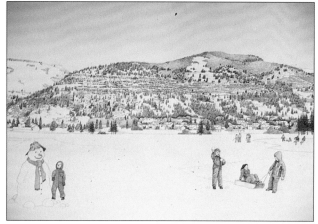

FROM ABOVE L TO R: Resort Development at Telluride, Colorado, Derek Walker Associates – view of development including man-made lake; winter season: skiing and sledging; resort development; summer season: golf and sailing

OPPOSITE FROM ABOVE L TO R: Resort Development at Telluride, Colorado, Derek Walker Associates – detail of housing fingers; lake view; detail of hotel peninsular; plan of valley floor set in context

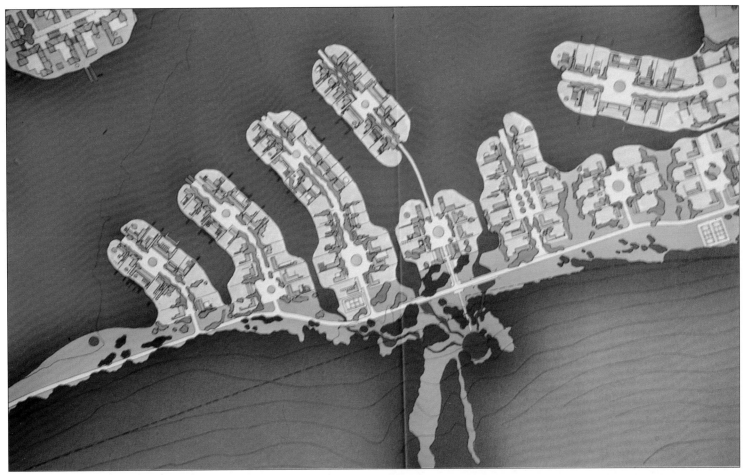

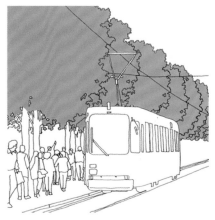

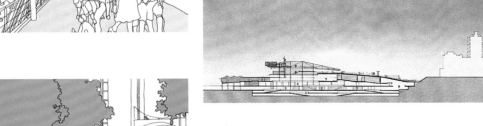

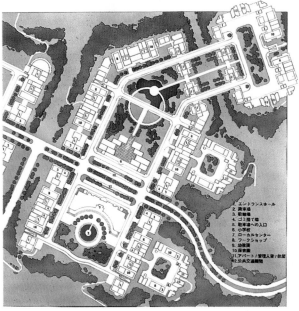

1. エントランスホール
2. 貴車場
3. 駐輪場
4. ゴミ捨て場
5. 駐車場への入口
6. 小学校
7. ローカルセンター
8. ワークショップ
9. 幼稚園
10. 保育園
11. アパート / 管理人室 / 住宅
12. 公共交通機関

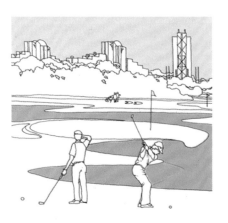

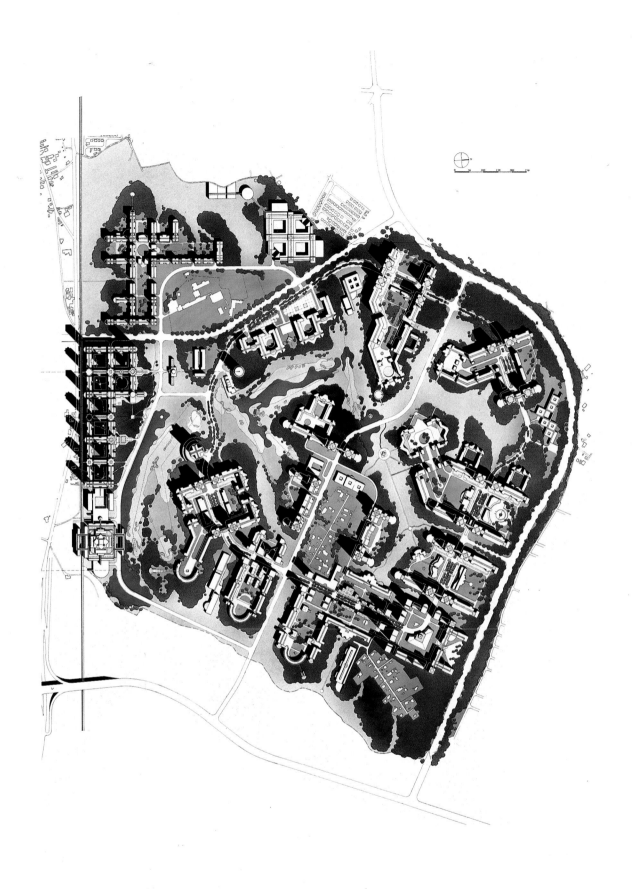

ABOVE: Forest Hills, Ushiku City – site plan showing housing and the public transport system which follows the internal road loop and links all residential areas to the retail/commercial complex beside the new rail station; OPPOSITE: Forest Hills: LEFT FROM ABOVE: Station interior; street scene; school; plateau gateway; CENTRE FROM ABOVE: Aerial perspective of site; section through railway station retail and leisure complex; station plan; typical housing area; RIGHT FROM ABOVE: Public transport; view from typical apartment; valleys for recreation and parkland with building on the plateaux preserving the hill edge and protecting the valley; PAGE 80 FROM ABOVE L TO R: Regeneration of Central Rotterdam, Derek Walker Associates – longitudinal sections through the Lijnbaan; Lijnbaan by night, perspective of covered street; road crossing; tram crossing; PAGE 81 FROM ABOVE L TO R: Longitudinal sections through the Lijnbaan; The Pipj, Amsterdam – elevation; section; master plan for Clarence Dock, Leeds, Derek Walker Associates; Royal Armouries Museum, Leeds, Derek Walker Associates

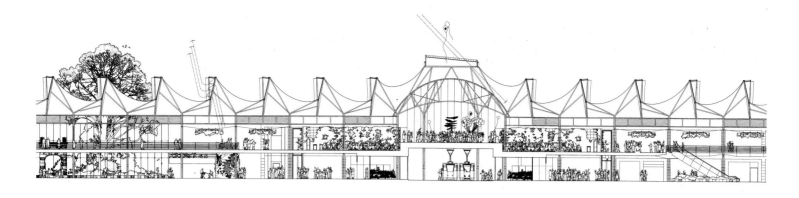

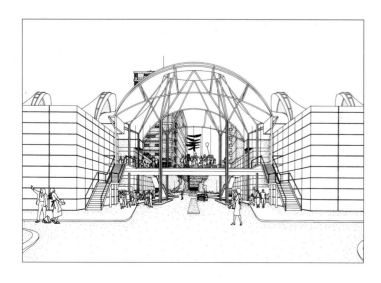

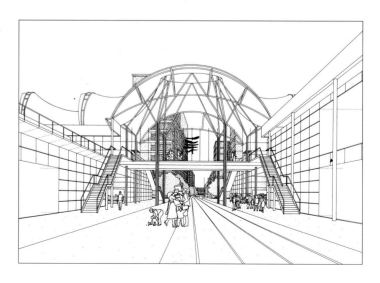

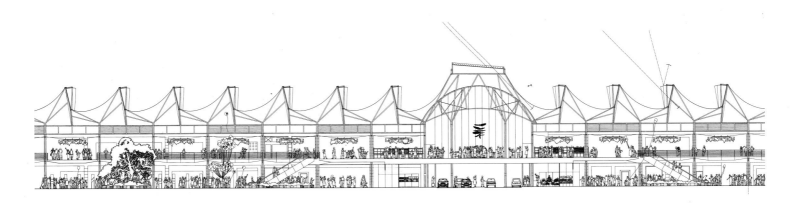

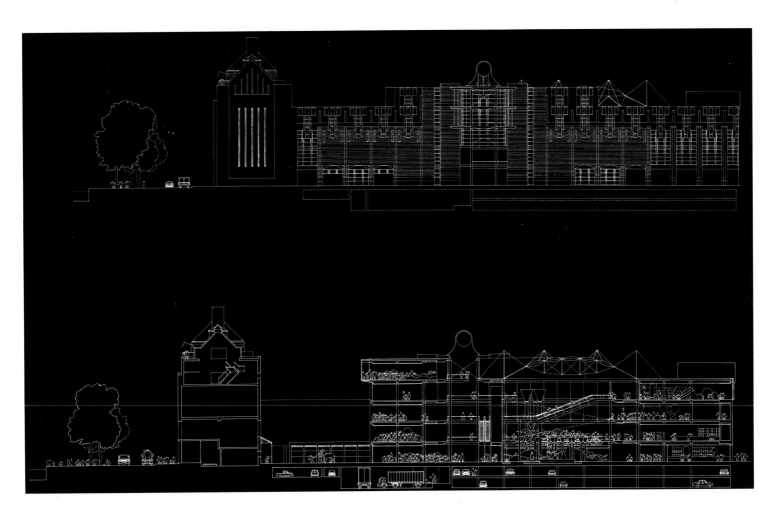

DAVID LOCK
THE LONG VIEW

Each New Town is founded for a purpose. In modern times the most common purpose is to accommodate the outward spread of cities in preference to sprawl: the majority of the UK government's New Towns have been founded for that purpose. At other times it might be to exploit a natural resource for industrial purposes; to act as an economic growth point; to retain populations in areas otherwise subject to exodus; for defence; for offensive purposes such as colonialism or imperialism; to provide a focus for government or civic activity; or to provide a haven for a religious or Utopian sect. It may be to fulfil the creative fantasy of a visionary individual, or simply to make money.

Milton Keynes was founded by the UK government in 1967 to fulfil the first of these objectives: to provide, in a planned way, for part of the overspilling population of London. Without another New Town in the northern sector of southeast England (there had been others before, such as Stevenage, Harlow and Hemel Hempstead), London's overspill threatened to swamp the leafy hills and green paddocks of the stockbrokers' dreamland in South Buckinghamshire.

The idea was promoted first in the early 1960s by Fred Pooley, the Chief Architect and Planning Officer of Buckingham County Council. With his architect/planner assistant Bill Berret, Pooley embellished the functional purpose of the new city with a personal creative vision of a place that would take the form of a high density cluster of neighbourhoods, joined by a rapid transit system.

The functional purpose of what became Milton Keynes was considered sufficiently important to be taken over by the government, who appointed a Development Corporation to implement it.

The Development Corporation rejected the Pooley vision of the place, and through a consultant team under the late Richard Llewellyn Davies, declared their own vision of a 'city of trees' in which the main component would be family houses with gardens, within an infrastructure that could cope equally well with private cars and public transport. Their vision was also of what we might now call an 'intelligent' city in which social and information networks would have an invisible geography – the realm of the 'urban non-place' as adviser Mel Webber called it – assisting the place to take on a third purpose, as a regional economic growth point.

Viewed internationally, the purpose of providing planned accommodation for metropolitan overspill is common enough. The vision of a 'city of trees' remains unique for a place created in a landscape previously devoid of significant tree cover, even in the present age of sustainable development when 'green cities' are commonly discussed. The idea of an 'intelligent city' did not emerge elsewhere, internationally, until the mid 1980s when the Japanese launched Kansai Science City in their own country, and in the late 1980s launched the Multi Functional Polis (MFP) in Adelaide, Australia.

The primary purpose of Milton Keynes was undone by the Labour government after 1976 when Environment Minister Peter Shore disconnected Milton Keynes' exclusive commitment to the overspilling population of London. Like other metropolitan politicians with successful New Towns over the horizon, he had become obsessed with the idea that Milton Keynes and the other New Towns were draining London of its most active people.

There are international precedents for government New Towns falling out of political favour in this way, though the reasons are never quite so facile. In the Ile de France region for example, Paris became disenchanted with its ring of New Towns in the 1980s. It had become clear that ordinary people considered them ugly, and only ethnic minorities and low income groups were willingly settling there.

In fact London, like other overblown industrial conurbations in the Western world, was repelling people anyway. The choice of a minority of the movers to go to the New Town, rather than ordinary suburbs and market towns, was not significant in numerical terms.

With its new brief generally to grow (rather than just to serve London), Milton Keynes Development Corporation cast its marketing campaign over a wider geographical area. This change of brief echoed that of Tama New Town in the Tokyo Metropolitan Region in the 1980s.

Following the election of the Thatcher government in 1979, the Development Corporation added to its vision of the place the idea that it might become an exhibition of the way in which market forces could be harnessed for a great public project. Viewed internationally, Milton Keynes is distinctive in this regard: while there

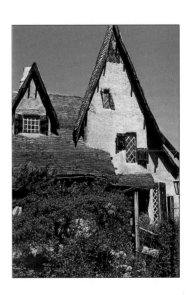

FROM ABOVE: Selling Letchworth; LA peep show, 'Witchville', Los Feliz; OPPOSTITE: City Armageddon, Fine Arts Squad, Los Angeles

FROM ABOVE L TO R: Welwyn Garden City; advertisement for Milton Keynes; Philadelphia, the proposition; Philadelphia, re-inventing the centre; Tama city, Japan – the long view; city centre

are private sector New Towns (such as Irvine, California, or even the original Garden Cities of Letchworth and Welwyn in the UK), for a public sector New Town to sustain its public purpose by using private investment to the extent achieved in Milton Keynes is unusual.

While market forces rapidly came to drive Milton Keynes, the Development Corporation could not hide the fact that it was a public sector project. If public projects were necessary, the Thatcher government preferred a tighter reign, and considered urban regeneration to be the national priority. Urban Development Corporations were established, using new legislation, and enjoying none of the planning, land acquisition and free-booting accounting freedoms of the New Town Development Corporations. Milton Keynes Development Corporation was told to dissolve itself in 1992.

Since then the Corporation has been replaced by the government's estate agents for unfinished New Towns: the Commission for the New Towns. The great public project of city building is almost entirely subordinate to the desire to sell the remaining real estate.

The city building skills of architecture, planning, social and economic development, landscape design and engineering have taken second place to the skills of real estate agents and accountants living far away. These cynical and exploitative talents had hitherto been rigorously controlled. The British way of finishing off its New Towns has always been odd when viewed internationally. To hand Milton Keynes over to the undertakers when it was only two thirds complete – and with many of its more challenging social and cultural facilities not yet created – is unprecedented. Members of the International New Towns Association consider it bizarre of the UK government to abandon such a promising town in its adolescence.

Size wise, Milton Keynes is 22,000 acres (8,900 hectares), with a current population of about 160,000, and a planned capacity of 250,000. There are around 1,000 New Towns around the world that have been started in modern times. The majority are relatively small (up to 50,000 target population), but in the decentralising metropolitan conurbations of the developed world, and the exploding city regions of the third world, it was common in the 1960s and 1970s to establish larger New Towns. Milton Keynes founded in 1967 at 250,000 can be compared with a number of contemporaries:

Cergy-Pontoise	(Paris region)	1966	350,000
Evry	(Paris region)	1967	455,000
Marne-le-Vallee	(Paris region)	1966	550,000
Melun Cenart	(Paris Region)	1965	291,000
Saint Quentin -en-Yvelines	(Paris region)	1967	480,000

Gandhinagar	(Gujerat, India)	1967	250,000
Chiba	(Tokyo region)	1967	340,000
Kashima	(Tokyo region)	1967	300,000
Kohhoku	(Yokohama)	1969	220,000
Cuidad Losada	(Venezuala)	1967	400,000
Almere	(Netherlands)	1970	250,000

The larger Paris New Towns were ambitiously huge for their time, and have been trimmed in size since. New town targets of that size are unusual: Brasilia, prominant in the lexicon of the international New Towns movement, had a target population of 500,000 when it was started in 1957, and was exceptional even for a putative national capital. Hong Kong's New Towns of the 1970s (such as Sha Tin, Tsing Yi, Tuen Min) were also targeted at half a million population, but the planning conditions in that small colonial enclave are also rare.

Milton Keynes was the last New Town to be started by the UK government, and is the largest. Until its focus was changed, Milton Keynes succeeded in its primary purpose of accommodating London overspill in a planned way. This was done without any kind of compulsion or financial inducements to industry, commerce or people: good jobs and houses were offered to people otherwise trapped in the inner city, and this was the main attraction, but Milton Keynes is unparalleled for its track record in also attracting the entrepreneurs and intellectuals who elsewhere in the world like to take advantage of New Towns but who, on the whole, would rather live some distance away.

As an exhibition of ways in which private sector resources can be employed in the creation of a New Town, Milton Keynes is distinguished internationally. The inventiveness of the late Development Corporation in finding ways of attracting private sector participation was startling: it was here, for example, that the concept of 'social housing' – discounted privately financed housing for low income households and those in housing need – was invented.

As a regional growth point Milton Keynes has been a success that stands comparison internationally. Sixty thousand jobs are located in the new city, a diverse local economy including both manufacturing and service sectors, relatively low unemployment levels even in the depth of the recession, and a conspicuous cluster of inward investment by companies from Japan, USA and Scandinavia.

Milton Keynes was developed by a special development agency created by central government and imposed on the locality. This agency, the Development Corporation, was empowered to acquire all the land for the project at 'no-New Town' values, and to borrow from central government (at two per cent above prevailing bank lending rates) to finance the scheme. Receipts

FROM ABOVE: Bofill at Cergy Pontoise (1977); Cergy Pontoise clock tower (1977)

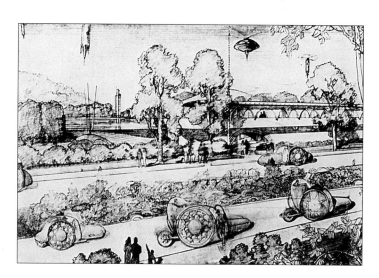

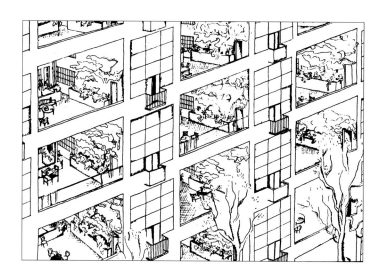

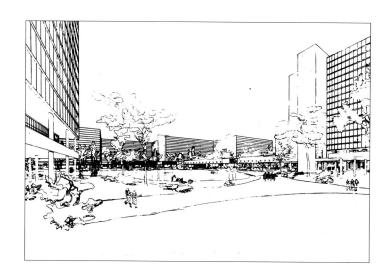

FROM ABOVE: Organic unity, Raymond Unwin's evocation of an idealised English village (1909); family living around the hearth, Unwin (1902); Broadacre City, Frank Lloyd Wright (1958); Broadacre City (1950) – cars and helicopters, Frank Lloyd Wright; Villa apartment, The Hanging Garden, Le Corbusier (1910-29); Radiant City, Antwerp, Le Corbusier (1933), not realised

from land and buildings provided the source of the return on the government's investment.

This technique of New Town building had been outlined by Ebenezer Howard in *Garden Cities of Tomorrow* in 1899, and experimented with in his privately funded projects for Letchworth Garden City (1903) and Welwyn Garden City (1921).

It is a technique that has been copied throughout the world, and is well proven, though the yield has never been as great as Howard expected (he envisaged the ability to be able to pay welfare and pensions from the yield, too), and a project of the scale and duration of Milton Keynes couldn't service the debt built up through the UK's inflationary 1970s and has had to be written off in part by the government (allowing the sneer 'Millstone Keynes' to gain currency).

Even where New Towns have been private sector projects – as with Irvine New Town in California – the approach to funding and organisation has been a reflection of the method outlined by Howard. Private sector New Town developers have found it inevitable that they should behave like public sector development corporations, though they enjoy the freedom to borrow from the commercial money markets at commercial rates, rather than from the government at punitive rates.

The vision of Milton Keynes as a green place – of trees, parks and gardens – is not uncommon in climates where green already exists (for example, Tapiola in Finland). However, the extent of afforestation designed and carried out in Milton Keynes on poor ground long cleared for agricultural use is exceptional. The extent and effect of the planting in Milton Keynes is not yet widely appreciated. It is growing through the city surreptitiously, and in 50 years the 'city of trees' idea will at last be visible, appreciated and lauded.

Unusual amongst public sector New Towns outside the UK is the basic building brick of the family house and garden. This is often inaccurately decribed as being a 'suburban' vision. It is, rather, a culturally correct design response to the essence of English tastes in living environments, and a pragmatic response to the need to attract residents, rather than (as has happened in the New Towns of Hong Kong or in a more obvious way in the New Towns of the former Soviet Union) simply accommodate those compelled to be there.

Also unusual is the way the grid is used in the master plan. Grids are a democratic division of the land (such democracy being unusual in England with its feudal history), and are common in New Town plans throughout world history. The grid is also the unique mark that man can make over the patterns of nature.

In Milton Keynes, reflecting more of a partnership with nature than a desire to dominate it, the plan of the city is a 'lazy grid' that responds to topography and accidents of geography. It is

also a 'supergrid' in that it is designed for cross-city movements and not for all movements. Only in Central Milton Keynes, and in some of the early public housing projects, is the grid applied in a conventional way.

A lazy supergrid as a transportation framework for a city was innovative when it was launched in 1967, in international terms, though, it was a logical extension of the way New Town plans had been evolving in England (in the Portsmouth/Southampton 'Solent City', and the GLC's still-born Hook New Town for Hampshire), and has been influential internationally ever since (for example in Abuja, the Federal Capital, and Asaba the new Delta State capital, in Nigeria).

The integrity and continuity of the city's linear park system is a conspicuous feature of the plan for Milton Keynes. River valleys in which building is not possible, and where storm water attenuation lakes have to be located, are turned opportunistically into an amenity. The quantity of open public space in Milton Keynes is generous when considered internationally, but its inspired distribution as green/blue threads on which spaces and recreation facilities hang like beads has not yet been similarly carried off in subsequent New Town plans. The design anticipated the current desire, in the pursuit of sustainable development, for 'wildlife' or 'habitat' corridors in cities.

The dispersal of employment areas in Milton Keynes is another major feature of the master plan. While each area can be caricatured as a form of zoning, and therefore the antithesis of mixed use, this is to misunderstand the scale of things. Employment areas, through being dispersed throughout the city, are close to neighbourhoods: short of compelling people to live next to factories, as urban design zealots would have other people do these days, the proximity of home and workplace in Milton Keynes can be as close as you choose.

The dispersal of employment areas also exploits the freedom of the supergrid, and eliminates the rush hour stampede to and from neighbourhoods which is still common in most of the world's New Towns. It has also given the city a portfolio of sites of widely differing character, and this has proved to be a marketing advantage.

Viewed internationally today, Milton Keynes must be assessed against the concept of sustainable development, the subject of international treaties at the Earth Summit at Rio de Janeiro in 1992. More than 100 nations signed Agenda 21, a 500 page document committing them to the pursuit of sustainable development, defined as: 'development that meets the needs of the present without compromising the ability of future generations to meet their own needs.'[1] At an EU sponsored conference at Aalborg in Denmark in May 1994, the concept was made the subject of a Charter for Sustainable Towns and Cities, to

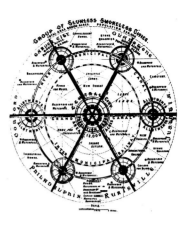

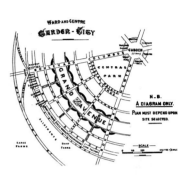

FROM ABOVE: The Social City, six garden cities connected by canals and railways from Tomorrow *(1898); one slice of the circular pie, a typical ward and centre of the garden city, Ebenezer Howard (1902)*

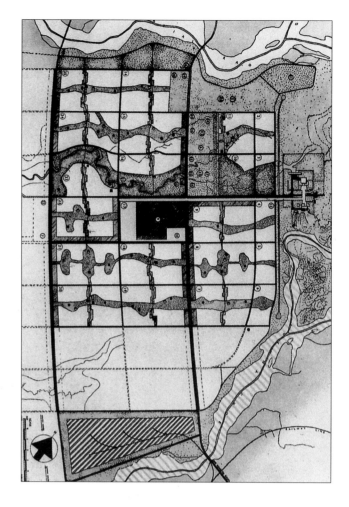

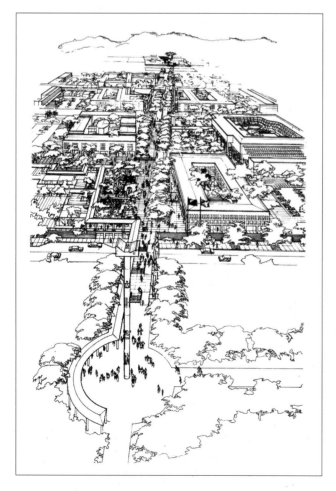

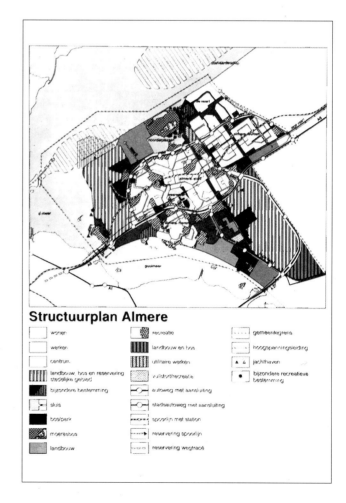

Structuurplan Almere

which municipalities from all over Europe have formally subscribed.

Given that urban development was required, Milton Keynes took land that was of poor agricultural quality. Its afforestation is likely to exceed that required to absorb the greenhouse gases generated by its development. Its densities and 'supergrid' have so far made public transport services expensive and therefore inadequate, which is a major failing, but the private cars on which the city depends at present run efficiently, and use less fuel and create less pollution per passenger mile than such vehicles in ordinary towns. There is a network of neighbourhood footpaths and cycleways of which the city is proud, though most New Towns throughout the world have made similar provision (though, admittedly, to a lower specification than that found in Milton Keynes).

Since 1986, when Milton Keynes Development Corporation created The Energy Foundation, Home Energy Rating, and the promotional event 'Energyworld', the city has been outstanding in reducing energy consumption. It has not ventured into Combined Heat and Power (CHP), however, despite many opportunities in planning new sections of the town, and in that regard is primitive when compared with New Towns in Scandinavia. Arrangements to collect methane gas at the city's sewage works (it was originally envisaged this might be used for the city's buses and taxis) is run to waste, as nobody could be bothered to follow through with the idea. Neither have special efforts been made to encourage the use of 'environment friendly' building materials, to discourage the use of tropical hardwoods from unsustainable sources, or to discourage equipment using CFCs which damage the ozone layer.

No special efforts have been made to minimise water consumption, though metering experiments are underway. Construction has not involved much waste of topsoil, as this has been regarded as a precious commodity, though subsoils have been disturbed in the city centre, especially where large flat footprints have been selected for major buildings, and some underground service roads and accommodation created.

Quantities of waste generated in Milton Keynes are typical of the UK, but waste handling is very sophisticated: the Community Recycling Opportunities Programme (CROP) organises separate household collections for various forms of recyclable waste, which are processed in a large factory opened in 1994, though commercial waste still goes straight to landfill along with residual household and garden waste: there are no incineration facilities.

There are other tests inherent in sustainable development against which Milton Keynes might be assessed, but its deliberate design to act as a regional growth point warrants mention. Both as a result of being freed from an exclusive relationship with London, and the vaulting ambition of its Development Corporation, Milton Keynes has deliberately sought to attract people from up to two or three hours travelling distance for leisure, shopping and employment. This persists to this day, as further extension of the shopping building is being contemplated.

Setting up this kind of magnet is no longer appropriate in a world where unnecessary travel by private car is to be discouraged. Rail and coach access to Milton Keynes is excellent north-south, but appalling east-west: since Rio, it might reasonably be argued that improvements to the latter should be a precondition of the development of further regional attractions in the city.

In a symposium in Tokyo in 1993, comparing Tama New Town with Milton Keynes, my Japanese colleagues agreed there were several different phases in the development of a New Town. First there is the practical phase, in which the engineers install the physical requirements of the city such as the first highways and drainage systems. This phase is soon over, though it disrupts the lives of the farmers and other people who lived in the area before, and who often become very angry to see the countryside changed in such a dramatic way. They wonder if the New Town will ever really happen. This phase is like preparing the ground in a garden, before the seeds are planted.

Second, there is the pioneering phase, when the first housing projects are constructed. New residents are at first delighted with their new homes – it must have seemed like paradise! – but soon become tired of the mud and noise from construction activity around them, and wonder if the New Town will ever be finished. This phase is like the moment when the first seedlings appear in the new garden.

Third is the consolidation phase, when there are sufficient new residents for the New Town to begin to have its own civic and cultural life. It is the phase when the number of small children exceeds the number of grown-ups. At this point people are a little critical of the New Town, as they are impatient to see the diversity and variety that should be expected in such a large community. This is like the period in the garden when new plants and trees make strong growth.

Fourth is the phase in which the New Town begins to blossom: the New Town develops its own sense of identity and starts to compete with other towns in attracting new investment, and in sports and in other areas of activity. Cultural and entertainment facilities begin to develop, education and health care services widen in their scope, employment begins to grow in the town as companies are attracted to the location. Interest in the political life of the town begins to grow, and the amount of construction activity (and the noise

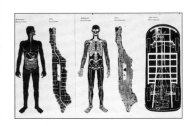

FROM ABOVE: Irvine, California, corporate cityscape; Man Transforms, *Hans Hollein, structure planning; OPPOSITE FROM ABOVE L TO R: Plan of Irvine; schematic plan of Chandigarh, capital of Punjab, India, Le Corbusier (1951); Dodoma, Tanzania, perspective of the centre, Conklin and Rossant, New York; structure plan of Almere, Holland*

ABOVE: Tapiola, city in a forest, Finland

and mud that it creates) begins to decline. This is a happy time.

Fifth is the phase in which the town bears fruit: its children have become adults – they are the 'second generation' of the New Town – and demand a home and a job in their own town. The pioneers start to join the silvering population, and make increasing demands for health services and other support systems. The residents have more sophisticated demands for entertainment, cultural and educational programmes, and the political life of the town becomes more lively. This is the phase in which people are proud to say that their New Town is home. They are aware that it is a place that has been carefully designed and planned to work well and look beautiful. They may no longer be very interested in all the hard work that was needed to make it happen, but they are aware that it is different to an ordinary town. They have high expectations for the future, they expect a good quality of life, and they are used to change in the world around them. This is the phase in which New Town becomes home town.

Milton Keynes and Tama were both created by a special development agency of national government. Milton Keynes was designed to accommodate overspill population from London, and Tama New Town has provided the same service to Tokyo.

Milton Keynes was started in 1967, and Tama New Town in 1964. The target population of Milton Keynes was 250,000. The target for Tama New Town was 300,000, since revised to 370,000. Now we come to a big difference: Milton Keynes is 8,900 hectares, whereas Tama New Town is 6,900 hectares. Allowing for the fact that part of the Tama New Town area cannot be built upon, because of topography and other physical constraints, it is clear that Tama New Town has been built at a much higher density than Milton Keynes.

This difference is because of the shortage of land in Japan, compared with the UK, which makes Japanese people more familiar with higher density living than are the British. However, building land in Britain is becoming more scarce. We are also becoming more concerned to use less energy and give less room to cars in our lives and our landscape, so that our densities are rising. As people in Japan become more wealthy, they are demanding lower density living. Perhaps in one more generation the living densities of the two countries will start to converge.

As in any international comparison, there are numerous similarities and stark differences. But common to both Tama and Milton Keynes, and a challenge to all New Towns in any part of the world as they near completion of their original master plan, is the transition from New Town to home town.

In making the transition the role of the town planners and city builders must become less, and the role of the residents must grow more and more.

It is necessary, and desirable, that the citizens of the New Town should take more responsibility for their own town: by taking part in the life of the town through its societies, institutions and political organisations. The mood must change from being (to parody the words of JF Kennedy) 'what can the New Town do for me?' to become instead 'what can I do for my town?'

This is the challenge, and the opportunity, that faces the people of Milton Keynes and, sooner or later, of all New Towns. The city builders must let go, and we residents must learn to make our towns more diverse, productive and conducive to a good quality of life. Excellent foundations may have been laid, but the future is now in our hands. That is an obligation that transcends local, national and international boundaries.

1   *Our Common Future*, Report of The World Commission on Environment and Development (The 'Brundtland Commission'), 1987

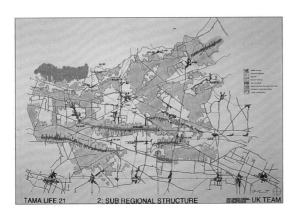 

ABOVE: Tama City, Japan; LEFT: Tama life, sub regional study, David Lock Associates (1990)

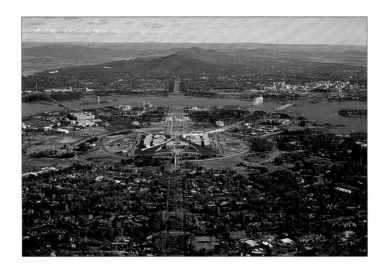

Canberra National Capital of Australia – National Capital Planning Authority (international competition won in 1911 by Walter Burley Griffin of Chicago); FROM ABOVE L TO R: View from Mount Ainslie; parliamentary triangle; Floriade Flower Festival; The Carillon; High Court of Australia; lakeshore cycleway

Lifestyles – ABOVE: The American dream – Malibu and sweet LA; CENTRE: The French variation, Place des Vosges and Marne la Vallée; BELOW: The British back garden, Heelands by Larsen and Castlefield by Gosling; PAGE 94: The Future – idyllic floating cities or more of the same concrete and carbon monoxide. Sid Mead and

Cal Tran provide the options. One manageable the other unattainable. The classic dilemma . . . PAGE 95: Kansai, the floating worlds of Japan . . . an airport city terminal by Renzo Piano/Ove Arup & Partners – FROM ABOVE: the island base; the airport structure

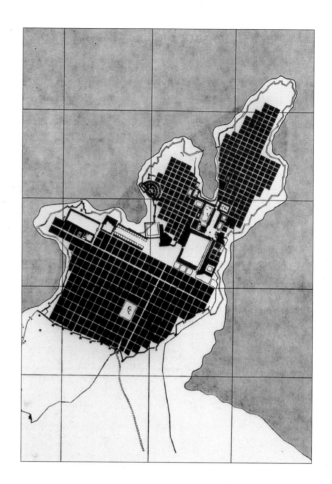

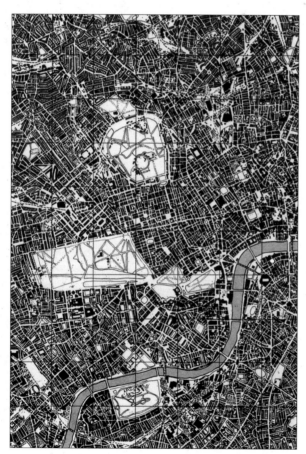

*The structure of cities – FROM ABOVE L TO R: Kyoto,
Japan (AD 794); Miletus, Greece (4 BC); London,
England today; Paris, France today*